Table of Contents

Preface 1

January 3

February 6

March 21

April..42

May 45

June 58

July 70

August 74

September 89

October.. 105

November.. 115

December 119

The Australian characters.................................... 122

The overseas characters.. 136

The issues.. 142

Barracking from the Sidelines 2015

(My personal political commentary on politicians and political events in 2015)

By Greg Tuck

Preface

Australian Politics

Dominated by a federal government, in a three-tier system of government, Australian politics is based on a constitution written in the 1890's that is extremely difficult to change via referendums. It is a Westminster system of government that has two separate chambers that are dominated by two major parties whose ideologies differ and both the sides are very combative to the extent that agreement on issues except politician wage increase, are hard won battles. If one side thinks of an idea, the other side shoots it down in flames, whether the idea is good or not. The public have become disillusioned and feel impotent to change things and see most politicians as merely sucking on the public teat and lining their own pockets. A good few of the political rank's behaviour does nothing to dispel that idea.

Politics changed a lot in Australia from late 2013 onwards, although many will attest to the fact that it hasn't changed at all. There are still lies, deception, obfuscation and manipulation and these have had to become more sophisticated as social media has come to the fore. I have been adding my own comments to mainstream media and my own political blog in those years and on reflection I am amazed at the types of characters that are regularly unearthed and come to the forefront in our political climate.

Some characters have developed over that time. Some were just fleeting shadows on the political spectrum. Others rose from obscurity and some may have also have faded back into it. Characters and events overlap. Views change and political manoeuvres take place. Ideology dictates much of what goes on. Hopefully my blog entries and reflections will help paint a picture of these characters and events that dominated the political scene in this period. This is not a chronological history of the time, merely one person's thoughts that he wanted to scream at the major players in Australian politics at the time.

However, the disappointing thing about all these comments and research is what I still really don't understand is, how does the Canberra bubble still remain intact with so many pricks in it? Are there special properties of moral vacuums?

January

- Major bushfires in Adelaide Hills. $4 million Federal funding allocated.
- Federal Health Minister, announces that the proposed $20 cut to rebates for short consultations with GPs announced in budget will no longer happen
- Tony Abbott "knights" Prince Phillip
- The High Court of Australia rules that the Federal Government acted legally in detaining 157 Tamil asylum seekers aboard a Customs boat
- A series of massacres in Baga, Nigeria and surrounding villages by Boko Haram kills more than 2,000 people
- Al Qaeda terrorists kill 12 people and injure 11 more in Paris

"The definition of stupidity is doing the same thing over and over again and expecting different results." — Albert Einstein. So, what would Albert think of Tony continually making the same mistakes and apologising for them?

Bad judgement calls by a PM have potentially more dire consequences than just a bad line call in tennis. The PM is the person who can, in effect, commit and send our troops off to another war. I am sure that people in Australia would prefer a PM who so frequently didn't say ..."oops".

It looks like Tony is following the path of the character of the author he probably perceives as yet another great knight, Sir Vantes. Tony, the new Don Quixote, is living in a fantasy world of his own creation and tilting at windmills. To get a second term now seems like an Impossible Dream.

With apologies to Paul Kelly
"In a muddle, in a muddle, in a muddle it does seem
He's lost the plot, knighted almost kings.

He's done all the dumb things"

Rosie Batty is a victim but she wasn't awarded Australian of the Year because she was just a victim. It was what she did afterwards. She could have sat back and cried "woe is me". Instead she has battled to raise the awareness of Australians of the dangers and reality of family violence. This is why many of us honour this special Australian. Many of our true heroes have shown that by rising above adversity much good can be achieved and change can occur. Hopefully critics won't denigrate this worthy recipient or the award itself. We already have a Prime Minister who is doing that with conferring of one knighthood in particular.

Sir Prince Phillip does have a ring to it, albeit an anal ring. So "out of date" doesn't just mean archaic. Tony Abbott has just given Bill Shorten's well-timed republican push a huge boost. It seems that Tony sees a good idea and decides the best thing to do is do the direct opposite. He must be living in an alternate universe. Is giving a knighthood to Prince Phillip a demotion?

With apologies to Sam Cooke's version of "What a wonderful World"

Don't know much about the economy
Shirt fronting is my foreign policy
The Human Rights Commissioner is a sook
Don't want you to see a GP when you're crook
Well climate change is a lot of crap
And Chrissie Pyne's such a lovely chap
Remember all Australia elected me
Don't know much about geography (where's Canadia?)
I hide the scar of my lobotomy
Don't know why I'm not popular
But Bronnie thinks that I'm a shooting star
Joe is nearly sure one and one is two.
After that he's confused, me too

The Cabinet have pledged their love for me
Now I don't claim to be a Rhodes scholar
But I am you see
In Oxford as a Rhodes scholar I learnt
How to fake sincerity
So I blame Labor for the economy
But my captain's calls are all at sea
Remember that I stopped the boats
Rupert's press keeps me afloat
Decision making, well I haven't a clue
I made a knight out of a duke
But I ingratiated myself with royalty
La ta ta ta ta ta ta
(Duplicity)
Ooh ooh ooh ooh ooh ooh
(Autocracy)
La ta ta ta ta ta ta........

Has the Abbott government gone to the dogs? You remember the cartoon of the dogs playing poker? What if the dogs were having a cabinet meeting instead? Tony would be the aggressive pitbull, Christopher the snappy irritating little terrier, Malcolm the intelligent border collie, Julie the feisty smart poodle, Warren the recumbent bloodhound, Barnaby the bellicose blue heeler, Scott the hard working German Shepherd, Peter the dutiful spaniel, George the argumentative pug, and then there's Joe the basset hound who officially "has little ability to adapt to situations and learn new things. He is actually a happy, friendly soul with comical antics".

February

- Prime Minister Tony Abbott announces that the Federal Government is abandoning its paid parental leave proposal.
- RBA makes official cash rate 2.25 per cent, an historic low
- A United States Court Review strikes down Australian David Hicks' conviction for supporting terrorism
- Major cyclone hits Northern Territory and North Queensland
- Social Services Minister Scott Morrison releases report recommending that the current child care system be abolished and replaced with a single subsidy available to nannies "to better meet the needs and budgets of families"
- Tony Abbott plans to strip Australian citizenship from dual nationals found to be involved in terrorist acts
- Tony Abbott uses VIP jet to fly from Canberra to Sydney for a 20-minute press conference during a Parliamentary sitting week
- Joe Hockey proposes an application fee on foreign investors wishing to purchase established homes.

Tony has issues with grammar. He confuses what he "can do", "will do", "promise to do", "wants to do" and "what is doable". Sounds like his problem is also with do - do's.

Tony needed a great speech today. Not only to inspire us as a nation but to protect his back in the party room. This was no Redfern speech, no "light on the hill". Obama, Kennedy and Churchill gave speeches that command attention. Tony shows he has lost command.

He has missed the opportunity to set a new course or hand over the con, so it looks like the Captain will go down with the ship. How many rats will scamper to safety?

He stopped the boats, killed the mining tax and carbon tax and is cutting the deficit. Core promises indeed just like no cuts to the ABC and SBS, introduction of Paid Parental Leave, no cuts to Health and Education.............. or were these non-core commitments? I don't understand polispeak. It sounds gibberish me,

I think that the actors in today's political theatre are being overpaid and are underperforming. Is it a drama or a comedy? If I don't like the show, am I allowed to get up and walk out? Can the taxpayer ask for a refund? Or does the show have to go on?

The light seems to have gone out on what is becoming the coalition train heading for a train wreck. How many politicians does it take to change a light bulb?

Tony's going great! Or should that be Tony's going; great!

Picture this: Julie and Tony singing "The Two of Us"...... People talk, they smile and say they know it won't last, we're holding on fast to a dream, we don't know what they mean........

I can't stand the suspense. Just who will be our leader? Michael Clarke, Steve Smith or George Bailey?

"This is just a media blow up and press speculation"........... Sorry was just reading yesterday's Lib Party script.

Misread headline "Lib's pill bitter and hard to swallow" or "Lib spill bitter and hard to swallow". You choose......

Young Christopher wouldn't have said such a thing. If he did, he would be speaking <u>S</u>howing <u>H</u>is <u>I</u>rrational <u>T</u>houghts. That's the way he always speaks. *(In response to Pyne's comment to Albanese "<u>C U Next Tuesday</u>")*

On a separate topic but worthy of note. Tony Abbott asked the people of Victoria to use the Victorian election as a referendum on the East-West tunnel project. The voters have spoken and he now all but calls us stupid. What is worse however is the Liberal Party's sanctioning of corporate greed. "From little things big things grow" The residents of Marysville in Victoria look like getting $300

million to share as compensation from a private company for loss of life, having their houses destroyed and their lives threatened and turned upside down in the Black Saturday bushfires. A private company will get about $1 billion from the Victorian government for holding the previous government to ransom over the contracts for the East-West Link. One has waited six years and the other will probably wait six months. Compare the pair as the ad suggests.

If we keep tossing out Prime Ministers no-one will want the job. Would we be better off with no-one? Perhaps that is the solution. Elect a group of people who will all work together in the best interests of Australia. No parties, no leaders..... might be worth a go.

There is an even more real reality show waiting to be produced. It will be filmed on Manus Island and should be called "I'm a Refugee. Get me Outa Here"

You'd think that Tony might not have just watched, but also have learned from the musical chairs game that Labor played when it came to the throne of PM. Every so often the music would stop and someone sat down while another person would blow up the dynamite that was attached to the chair. Then the music would start again, the game would continue until all were mortally wounded. Tony, who marches to the beat of his own drum now sits in the chair, but has also found the detonator and hasn't stopped to consider what would happen if he pushed the wrong buttons. You don't need to be a Rhodes scholar to work out what would happen. In fact, it obviously helps if you aren't.

Has Captain Tony forgotten that shooting yourself in the foot whilst it is still in your mouth is tantamount to suicide, especially political suicide?

"Blue ties will certainly cheer up
If Tony can be replaced
Or else they will end up rear up
An opposition in disgrace
Spread smiles on every Australian face

And put a new PM in place."

If you are hoist by your own petard is it painful? Will Tony have to see a doctor about it? I am sure many like me would pay his GP co-payment for him.

If an abbot and two bishops lose their jobs, is that religious persecution?

Speaking of military stuff. To cut pay to the armed services is an act of contempt. Wage freeze would be bad enough but to send our troops overseas into conflict and tell them that that an assessment has been made of the value their life is worth and it is now worth less than it was a year ago is arrogant detachment. Perhaps all politicians should do some front-line combat duty to assess what for our defence force are their workplace conditions. Hopefully they will wear their regular high vis vests when they do.

Would Malcolm be better off waiting 18 months and when the election is lost, accede to everyone's pleas to become leader? If he gets the job, now he may find himself leading this mob to an election loss anyway, although less catastrophic. And then the knives will be out for him.

Did Joe intimate that Tony had the full support of the board. In Aussie Rules footy parlance that tells the coach he is about to be sacked.

In the party room tomorrow we will hear, "Aye, Aye, Captain" if the PM asks for a confidence vote. For him, sadly that means "I think the nays have it".

Tony out and about. Is he looking for deck chairs? His job after tomorrow if he wins may mean rearranging them.

Campbell Newman was so confident about the party's direction and his leadership he called an election. Go for it, Tony. Experiencing the unemployment queue may make you a more rounded individual.

The whole thing is a game to these people. Schoolyard bullies in a gang, mentality jockeying for one-upmanship in a petty quarrel about whose anatomical appendage is bigger.

Names and initials. We all know what BS stands for. TA is an acronym for Trades Assistant - someone who learns on the job, but often is not quite up to the task. Malcolm's is MT which sadly means vacuous.

We didn't vote for Tony we voted for a person in our own electorate to represent us. The majority elected were Liberal and National party. The Liberal party elected members chose Tony, not us. We had no say.

Was Abbott heading down to Bondi in his red budgie smugglers to further bury his head in the sand? The tide of public opinion is against him.

Maths says that the spill vote didn't go ahead because of twelve people. If another twelve had said yes instead of no then a spill would have occurred.

This morning was a right royal stuff-up. No...... that was giving Prince Phillip a knighthood .... or actually bringing back knights and dames in the first place. So that makes this morning just a right stuff-up..... and now we just continue to lurch further and further to the right. They'll be having a Tea Party soon. They're all as mad as hatters, or is that Katters.

Someone should tell Joe in case he is asked "What is the capital of Australia?" that the answer is Canberra and not $2.57 because Labor spent all the rest. That is his usual line.

"Good government starts today." That's interesting as Abbott promised at the last election "better government". It is good grammar 101. Good is an adjective, better is the comparative adjective and best is the superlative adjective. So that would make the previous government the best and his own government on the downward slide to bad, worse, worst.

Why is it called "Question Time" when no-one answers what is asked? Those in government insist that they have all the answers too.

Rupert's on the outer with a Saudi prince so what does he need? Perhaps another company tax cut? It is probably just a coincidence that Tony announced one.

The bells are ringing for Parliament but for whom the bell tolls? It tolls for thee Mr Abbott.

Phone call to Mike Baird.

"Hello Chief. This is Max. There is still Kaos out there but Tony is still in Control. They missed him by "that much". Sorry 'bout that Chief."

Will the Ides of March be a little bit early this year? See what daylight saving does to things!

Just how far to the right beyond Attilla the Hun is Cory?

Will this new reality show be called "The Biggest Loser" or "I'm the Prime Minister. Get me outa here!"

There was concern about the need for firearms in Parliament and many thought that only if a clear and present threat existed. So my question is "Would a spill motion count as a real and present threat?"

Is anyone running a book on how many MP's will be tossed out by Bron this year? I severely underestimated last year and was out of the running early. Have learnt my lesson.

How many new life-saving drugs could have been put on the PBS; how many refugees could have been processed; and how many new renewable jobs could have been created in the time that has been devoted to the internal navel gazing of this government in recent weeks?

Is this Government, like my poetry, going from bad to verse?

Our very own Rip Van Winkle, Tony Abbott, has been asleep at the wheel for a long time. He thinks he is still back in the fifties.

Will Campbell Newman now move to Northern Victoria to begin wooing support for a tilt at the big house in the electorate of Indi? Apparently, he thinks everything governmental should be up for sale including a seat.

Amazing how security has been beefed up at parliament at the same time as financial, employment and social security in the general population has dropped markedly. Coincidence???

Was the vote count yesterday done by Joe Hockey? You know he can't manage numbers. Tony may have actually been in deficit.

The press may be ambulance chasers, but they don't create the accidents. I think Tony's minders have 000 on speed dial.

Tony has got the majority of his party behind him with promises of SA built subs still an option. If I was Tony however, I think the free set of steak knives they got with that gift was not a wise move. Watch your back, Tony!

I've got my money (not my house, Barnaby) on Andrews for the informal. It was his way of saying I want Abbott and Gillard back.

To the tune Groovin' by the Rascals
Losin', it's what we're about to do
Vic., Queensland and soon New South too
I can't see things getting any better
As long as this cabinet all stick together
Backbench ain't the place to be, soon I'll be
Losin', in my electorate too
Going backwards with nothing I can do
We all tried our best to get rid of Tony
To save face one voted informally
But can't beat cabinet solidarity
Losin', because they can call the tune
Queueing, at Centrelink all too soon......

The Japanese have come up with a design for a robotic submarine already that Tony is happy with after signing the trade deal. It is called the Abe-bot. (sounded better in my head but then again that's Tony's style of speaking too.)

I really don't understand politicians. They have to stand to get elected and having stood and won they get a seat and get to sit in judgement on legislation. They protect their seat at any cost, in any way so we then don't know what they stand for anymore. Backbenchers don't stand out or they might lose their seat. Now today a whole lot of them stood up and walked out. Perhaps many of them will be standing in dole queues shortly.

I am extremely disappointed that Russell Broadbent who is the member representing me chose to walk out during the opposition leader's response to the handing down of the Closing the Gap report today. It showed a lack of courtesy especially when this should be a bipartisan issue. Even if he disagreed with the contents of the response it signals to the aboriginal community and the wider community that this particular report is of little concern to him and as such the people of the McMillan electorate. How do I explain that to my aboriginal friends?

Government and parliament are different. Under the Westminster system, people are elected to Parliament. A leader who commands the majority in the lower house can with the Governor-General's consent form a government made up of members that he or she chooses. That group becomes the government. It is a shame and sheer waste of talent that a prime Minister doesn't select the best people in Parliament to form government and only chooses those from his or her own party or a coalition.

Our Captain Ahab, Abbott, is having such a whale of a time with the sub issue. Perhaps he'll insist that the Japanese scientists who have experience with whales help the Japanese builders design white ones. Perhaps white elephant ones could be considered too.

Revenue = expenditure, is the way to balance a budget, Mr Costello. You balanced the budget from the mining boom and gave out welfare to middle and upper incomes to shore up your support base. With the GFC and the drop away in the mining boom "you picked a fine time to leave Lucille". Tell Joe that to balance the budget he mustn't cut both revenue and expenditure at the same time. It doesn't work. Basic economics 101. Perhaps Joe needs to go and do that course. I'm sure he can manage the repayments on ay HECS debt he gets.

So, Thursday is the last day of the week for our parliamentarians. Tony said that it was back to work Tuesday. Wednesday finished early so the parliamentarians could socialise. To my mind that makes a two and a half day week on five times the weekly average wage. So how much lifting and how much leaning are our parliamentarians doing? Perhaps the unemployment numbers could be reassessed after checking out how many actually turn up in the chamber, how long they stay, and whether they actually do or say something beyond tweeting and planning their next holiday.

With unemployment on the rise, Joe will still want to balance the books. His methodology is simple. Here is the amount available and here are the number unemployed. Divide the first by the second and this will be the dole payment. Yes, it is a savage cut to the leaners but the books balance.

What would Australian Immigration do if the Indonesian Government put the two condemned prisoners minus passports on a leaky boat and deported them on their way to Australia? Wouldn't that pose a question for the Immigration Minister?

The Human Rights Commission is a body separate from, but reporting to Parliament. The abuse and continued detention of children who are in effect under the care of the Department of Immigration, should always be investigated without political interference. Then if some wrong doing should have occurred;

under the Westminster system of accountability, the Minister should stand up and on behalf of all Australians take full responsibility. Others of more moral stature in the past have resigned for far less.

ISIS doesn't represent Islam and the majority of people who practice Islam. It is an extreme terrorist group that uses Islam as a means of recruitment. Does it follow the teachings of Islam? No.

Tony to the King, "We have problems with frozen berries. Do you have problems with frozen nuts...? Chris Pyne wanted me to ask you, but I don't know why"

Tony has a problem with data retention as he keeps forgetting what his minders say. But so too does Chris Bowen. What was the tax-free threshold?

With the spare Order of Australia now that Rolf Harris has been stripped of his, will Tony allocate one to King Harald?

"stronger prohibitions on vilifying, intimidating or inciting hatred"..... Isn't that what Tony was actually doing by mentioning Islam in his speech?

An abbot talking about preaching. Next, we'll have a bishop defending religious persecution in a foreign country like of the Palestinians in Israel

Tony's address on national security. "Be alarmed and alert!"

**Tony has turned over new leaf. It was a fig one on his head.......
Think about it!**

How is Phillip Ruddock's unfair dismissal case progressing at Fairwork Australia?

So, Prince Phillip was given advanced warning of his demotion to a mere knight. Bet the other Phil didn't get any when he was demoted from being a whip.

If what we are witnessing in the Chamber at the moment is reasoned debate by the best in the country, no wonder they are cancelling the census. The census may prove they are the best and that the average IQ of all Australians has dropped faster than the Aussie Dollar.

Parliamentary privilege shouldn't extend to the questioning of Gillian Triggs's character when she has presented a report scathing of both sides of Parliament. She should have the right of reply or at least whistle-blower protection.

Obama finishes his job about the same time as our next election. Can we parachute him in? As long as he doesn't come by boat and end up on Manus Island, we could end up with someone in Parliament who can lead.

"decisions of the ERC [expenditure review committee] are unanimous". (missing last two words "or else")

Perhaps a game of Mastermind would fill the void between sensible questions and answers. Today's subject: The meaning of words.

First question: metadata

Second question: hypocrisy

Third question: death throes

Fourth question: bipartisan

Fifth question: Human rights commission independency

Spot the leopard in the blue tie. Even his own cabinet knows he can't change.

There won't be a Royal Commission into the children held in detention. There will be so much mud (and worse0 sticking to both Labor and Coalition parties that they will be unrecognizable from each other at the next election.

Just what date in March are the Ides? I want to book a front row seat in the Gallery in the House of Reps.

If you don't like a report, discredit the author. Now why didn't I think of that when I was in High School?

So, who would George Brandis have as a non-partisan head of the Human Rights Commission? There are several unemployed Liberal State ex-premiers.

The mere mention of the words "terrorism" and "security" will boost any incumbent government in the polls. Look what it did for George W Bush

So, Senator Ian McDonald has not read the report of the Human Rights Commission because it is partisan. How does he know? Is he a free and independent thinker or a party hack who is more like a ventriloquist's dummy than someone representing his state?

"Triggs is out of her depth." You have gotta be kidding. Then what of Tony? He is on the bottom of the Marianas Trench at the moment.

Who leaked the metadata of those emails from the Liberal Federal Treasurer, Phil Higginson? Can't you smell the scent of a Royal Commission in the air? Perhaps Sir Prince Phillip could chair it.

Turnbull knows that Shorten's "attacks" are like being hit with a feather duster. It is the attacks that his own party is making on its own credibility that should be of great concern for Turnbull.

So far Morrison has said more mothers need to go back to work, young people need to get a job and the elderly should stay in the workforce. This all sounds great except there is a declining jobs market and unemployment is going through the roof.

Could Gillian Triggs please stand for election? We need people of substance who don't bully and refused to be bullied. Our standard of parliamentarians is actually preventing good, honest, practical and caring people entering politics.

Speaking of crime. There has been a concerted attempt to detain and arrest people smugglers. What happens to those people involved with budgies?

Will charges be brought against the Attorney General? Lucky, he has his escape route planned. A secret passage runs behind his bookcase!

Wouldn't it be great for politicians to visit places for more than a photo op. Arrive unannounced, without a press contingent and high vis. vest and get a sense of what reality and normality are. They only get to do that when voted out of office. Ironic isn't it?

As part of their child care policies will both sides of Parliament please start to care about the children in detention.

Whose turn is it for character assassination today? Is anyone running a book on it?

Russell Broadbent has had a name change and possibly gender too. Dorothy Dix now represents McMillan.

I think that the Minister for Women has outlawed the word mandate as being sexist. See he has done one thing positive in that role.

It seems that once every ten years now a government will come to their census.

"Our story is always consistent, it's always correct." Sounds like Tony hasn't changed at all except to swap feet in his mouth. Hope he has protection!

I know people, when they put something into their mouth, want to have a good idea about what protections come with that." I hear you can get a variety of flavours. Avoid the blueberry and raspberry ones, Barnaby for a while

Xenophobia is behind many of the current government policies. "We can't let asylum seekers in!" "Overseas buyers need to pay more to buy a house here." "Muslims aren't real Australians." "Send them back where they came from when we have finished destroying their country's culture, political system and basic infrastructure because it is different to ours." Makes you wonder how far further to the right Tony Abbott is from Pauline Hanson.

Abbott has decided to invest in locally produced movies. First one he has tied people to is "Fifty Shades of Blue"

Apologies to the Beatles and their Yellow Submarine, but......

"In Iraq where we're at war
There's limited access to the sea
So why the hell do we need
To invest in submarines
(Chorus)
We don't need to buy any more submarines
Got no use for submarines
But big boys toys are expensive submarines...........
Expensive submarines"

The so-called war on terror was supposed to make us safer. We consequently invaded Iraq only to find out that suddenly we are far less safe and that terror has hit the home-front. It is like throwing petrol on a fire to extinguish it. If only there was a Science Minister then he/she could explain the parallel.

The old "dog ate my homework" excuse Chris Moraitis has used will stop the AFP investigation; but not the public condemnation of the sleazy tactics of Brandis and Co. who would rather discredit an individual rather than examine the contents of the HRC report.

Think of all those subs we will need to have when we send more troops to Iraq.

I guess we will hear all those shoe puns again now. "Tony has failed to sink the Slipper". "He went boots 'n' all into Gillian Triggs." "Haven't those poor old soles got better things to do?"

Why not just one qualification to receive welfare? One size fits all. I mean this government has stereotyped all who receive welfare as "leaners". So, go to Centrelean and fill in one form that says you are a leaner. To qualify for any benefit, you would have to be a young unemployed, disabled elderly pensioner who is indigenous and a single parent and .... etc. Cost savings made by the government would be the entire welfare budget.

I think the Mr Men and Little Miss characters could take over from emojis except that Tony may have schizophrenia being Mr

Silly, Mr Grumpy, Mr Grumble, Mr Mean, Mr Muddle, Mr No, Mr Nonsense, Mr Rude, Mr Scatterbrain, Mr Stubborn and course Mr Wrong at the same time.

Can Tony please stop repeating himself, repeating himself. It is becoming annoying, annoying and contagious too

When will Abbott go? I'd plumb for the Ides of March whenever they are. Et tu brute?

I can't believe that SBS is being cut and money is going to Defence where they have trouble with subplots and the government spin needs subtitles.

It is the opposition's role to analyse the policies of the government and monitor the implementation of those. This is what Pyne, Abbott and co bleated when they were in opposition. They had to hold the government to account. Labor is doing the same. The time to offer up policies as an alternative government is when there is a possibility of that occurring round which is around election time. That's what the Abbott led coalition did; although you would have to admit that the policies, they went to the election are vastly different from what they are implementing now.

March

- Federal Health Minister drops plans to introduce a $5 GP co-payment
- Prime Minister Tony Abbott announces that Australia will send another 300 troops to Iraq
- Australian defence force personnel will receive a pay rise of two per cent per year due to Jacqui Lambie's lobbying
- Data retention laws are enacted requiring phone and Internet providers to store metadata for two years.
- Parliament passes law requiring its internet and mobile phone providers to store customer data for two years as anti-terror measure.
- Tony Abbott described Aboriginal people living in remote communities as a "lifestyle choice"

Last week it was a storm in a teacup and now the wind has been taken out of the Captain's sails by the fully-costed plan by Labor to recoup money from aberrant business tax payers. Does Tony have a wind problem? I'm sure there's medication for that.

Blue ties are a symbol of solidarity with the right-wing philosophy of Tony Abbott and now many of the Libs are wearing mauves and pinks. Perhaps they are heading back to the centre.

"Blue skies are starting to clear out
Could Tony be in disgrace?
Backbenchers begin to share doubts
Watch the smile leave Tony's face...."

Could someone please tell me why the word lie is a no-no in parliament? If someone has actually misled parliament, misquoted someone or actually told an untruth why shouldn't that person be called for it? Any one being called a liar could and should demand

proof. But to say it is unparliamentary is a lie in itself. Politicians lie all the time. You can't get elected if you don't.

The photo of Prime Minister's empty chair says it all. The music is still playing and no-one is sure who will sit in that one when it stops and for how long.

If only the Senate was allowed to censor and not just censure Senator Brandis, then the report contents and not all the attacks on an individual would have been the focus.

Would the new data retention proposals have saved Chris Moriatis's notebook?

Senator Brandis says the secretary of his department, Chris Moraitis, has his "entire confidence". If that was said to an AFL coach by the board of the club he would know he was about to be sacked. I hope Chris knows where the nearest Centrelink is.

Morality of politicians is not checked in at the entrance to the chamber but the party room. You would hope that as they represent you in parliament and they should use the chamber to do just that, but instead they will say they raised it in the party room to no avail. As a party first person they will meekly follow what the party/prime minister/cabinet decides.

With the reaction to the HRC report, what will be the government's reaction be to the report about child abuse in institutions? Will they do anything at all? Will they attack the chair if they don't like the report? Or will it be just written off as a church problem where there was a failure to excommunicate?

One of the things the general public doesn't know is where products are being produced anyway so they can't even choose. This was highlighted with Berrygate last week. Basic economics says buy the cheapest one. Conservative governments say that we must drive wages down to compete. Labor governments say we must protect workers. Both show a lack of understanding. They aren't up to advanced economics yet.

If Australians bought Australian made goods then jobs would be retained and created and our biggest area of government expenditure, welfare, would decrease and tax revenue would increase from more PAYE workers. The biggest dilemma governments face is what can be done to support Australian industries before they are not just endangered as they are now, but finally become extinct. Anti-dumping laws and increased duties seems a reasonable answer as well as clear labelling of all products regarding the source of material, where it is processed and packaged.

So how are our free trade agreements going? Not berry good last week. Why did we rush to sign them? Why would huge world powers sign an agreement with a small country like Australia if they weren't getting the better of the deal. It is a ludicrous idea that we will be the ones better off. What we have done is consigned Australia to merely a mining pit and a backup food supply farm. We have opened our manufacturing to unfair competition that will decimate any existing businesses and effectively prevent any new start-ups.

If we were brave enough we would increase protection against dumping (by the way Americans use the word "dump" to signify something else but may also be appropriate for some of our imports). We won't. It is unnatural for a minnow to attack a shark. It is also unwise and unsuccessful. Governments of different persuasions have sold us down the river and they have sold the river as well.

A censure motion is a slap on the wrist, nothing more. What we give asylum seekers is a bit more than a slap on the wrist. They have committed no crime, yet, young children included, they are incarcerated for an indeterminate length of time, stripped of human rights and forgotten. When Brandis, Abbott and co. attacked Gillian Triggs they forgot the forgotten children. How apt! All these politicians will get at worst is a "Tut. Tut. Don't do it again." Makes you proud to be an Aussie.... NOT!

Freedom of speech is a right but comes with responsibilities. The attack of freedom of speech that Abetz is using as defence of Brandis overlooks the responsibilities that Brandis had to use the right properly. He, in effect, called Triggs a liar and made the attack personal. Where were Triggs' rights then?

Someone tell Abetz the HRC's comment on the asylum seeker charged with domestic violence was merely explaining the law as it stands. If Abetz doesn't like the law he is well placed to change it.

Didn't think that I'd ever agree with Amanda Vanstone, but over the Gillian Triggs attack by the Abbott Government she said "The high ground was there for the taking, and Tony Abbott chose to stay down in the boxing ring."

Isn't it amazing that so many Prime Ministers and ministers plan overseas and interstate trips around sporting fixtures? Free airfare, free entry, free food and they get paid to attend. So many do it that it forces the food and entry prices up for we plebs.

There won't be a change in PM in the next couple of weeks. The poll today isn't the reason. The main reason is the proximity to the NSW election. To dump Tony Abbott would be seen as a panic measure and no bounce would come quick enough to impact on the election. Should the government fall in NSW Tony's goose, in proper kitchen cabinet style, is cooked. If the government in NSW is re-elected but without a comfortable majority, Tony's goose is thawed, basted and the oven is pre-heated and his goose definitely is stuffed. The carving time would be post budget and Hockey will be a side-dish.

I think if Australians were able to sue political parties for false advertising we could bankrupt them and put them out of business tomorrow. I'd like the laws changed to allow that to happen. I have to find a political party stupid enough to shoot themselves in the foot though to put the bill forward. But there's plenty of those to choose from.

Was that the rattle of sabres in the Cabinet room or the sharpening of knives?

Again with the "dead, buried and cremated". It isn't logical because once it is buried how do you cremate it without raising it once more? ...... Oh I see!

I like the way John Key pronounced the area in and round Iraq. He called it the "Muddle East". How strangely apt.

If Coalition is willing to bow to public opinion as they say (e.g. GP co-payments) then how many of us will it take to get them to bring our troops home out of the Middle East?

Let's hope the new subs leak far less than the Cabinet Room

Eight flags for a press conference about sending troops to Iraq. How many flags needed for caskets when they return? Don't send troops. Send subs!

To quote Edwin Starr in his song
"War, huh, yeah
What is it good for
Absolutely nothing
Uh-huh"
Actually, it does give you a boost in the polls.

Seems that politicians think like Collingwood football coaches in the AFL. If you are losing, the best way to gain your own momentum is to start a fight.

We also sent troops to Vietnam to "just help out". Someone remind me how that worked out.

Watch for the Medicare co-payment reappearing in the form of a regulation amendment not as a piece of legislation.

Clive Palmer has revoked the blanket abstention of voting by PUP senators because Abbott is back in control.

a) What is the definition of control?

b) Is he controlled?

c) Does he now have self-control?

d) Was he out of control?

Answers to the above are:

a) The answer to that can only be defined solely by the controller

b) Yes but the puppeteers are hidden and not very good

c) No but he's working on it

d) Yes and is more often than not as evidenced by the leather scuff marks on his tongue.

Can someone please explain how long it actually takes to process an asylum seeker. If you can play cricket or possibly represent Australia in any other sport you are fast tracked. Perhaps we should send all asylum seekers and potential immigrants to the Australian Institute of Sport for processing.

Malcolm is right "Prank text messages sent to MPs via their public emails do not constitute hacking." We get prank messages in our mailboxes from politicians around election time.

What I didn't understand from Tony's speech (10:45) is why he used the word "not" to confuse us with what he truly believes.

What we need in Canberra from politicians and journalists is clearer labelling. Journalists should be made to clearly differentiate actual reporting from opinion. Politicians should be made to label what they say as spin, lie, half-truth, myth, fabrication, rumour or fact.

What is with all the street signs in the Liberal Party room?

"Stop" (the boats)

"Right Turn Only"

"Yield (backbenchers)"

"No U Turn permitted"

"Slow"

"Bumps ahead"

"Children (overboard/in detention/forgotten)"

"Keep Right"

And the sign that many can't see "Dead End"

The Minister for Women is too busy arranging the deployment of the sons and daughters of women overseas into dangerous locations.

The Minister Assisting the Prime Minister for the Status of Women, Michaelia Cash, will announce a new government plan to tackle workplace equality. I don't suppose anyone will ask them about the Cabinet Room?

Can Annabelle Crabb please keep an eye on Joe cooking the books? Sounds like the upcoming budget could be a recipe for disaster.

How many flags does it take to say you were wrong?........ A whole lot of invisible ones.

At least with a tiny pay-rise we can see that those troops overseas putting their lives on the line now know that their lives are worth a little bit more than bugger-all.

Many of the issues the Middle East have come about because of the European penchant for wanting to divide up areas of land based on what they perceive are in the best interests of themselves, not of the populations within the countries. This is why you get small enclaves of cultural groups trapped inside one country or whole groups of people who have no country like the Kurds. Afghanistan is not one country. It is actually a range of different cultural groups bound together by merely lines drawn on a map. look at what Europeans did to India and Pakistan. The unworkable solution i.e. the creation of Israel for the Jews thus disenfranchising Palestinians was caused by NIMBY. The sooner we "civilised" countries stop imposing our carving up of countries we have invaded the better. We are no good at it.

The point I am trying to make is that considered reasonable and rational responses come from Julie Bishop and Tony Abbott seems to not have his finger the pulse when it comes to subtle negotiations with overseas nations. I would prefer Julie rather than Tony to have her finger on the trigger when it comes to troop deployment .

Is there some sort of mechanism in Parliament House that sucks the morality, wisdom and the sense of fairness out of the politicians that say they will represent us?

The government has backed down on Medicare GP co-payment because they couldn't get broad support from the community. With Tony Abbott having had the least support of Prime Ministers from the community according to the polls why haven't the government changed their mind about him?

"He's a very intelligent, courageous, brave man, a very thoughtful guy. He's got a wonderful self-deprecating sense of humour." Yes, but Malcolm is Tony any good at his job?

People couldn't find a way around "the brick with eyes" (Glen Lazarus) on the field. Christopher Pyne is having the same problem in the Senate.

Andrew Chan's or Myuran Sukumaran's case really highlights the difference between "All Guns Blazing Rambo Abbott" and "Gentle but Firm, Diplomatic Julie". Wouldn't you prefer Julie to be making Captain's Call when it comes to important overseas issues such as troop deployment and helping those Australians overseas in trouble?

The Bali nine are receiving far more coverage and more government assistance than the Balibo five ever did. Same two countries but different era and totally different sides of the legal divide.

Eight flags yesterday as troop deployment announced. How many at half-mast during that deployment?

Tony Abbott's comments about the role Clive Palmer has in telling what PUP senators should do could backfire as that is what he does as leader of his party to his colleagues in the House of Reps. Trying to split the litter with a sledge hammer should be cause for the RSPCA

(Royal Society for the Protection of Carnage from Abbott) to be called in.

I think that the camera locations should be hidden and always change in Parliament. That way we wouldn't get all that posing for the camera that goes on, and playing to it like some ham/sham actors do.

Again, Malcolm seems to show that he has a positive voice and can show a vision. Is his role now mentoring Tony as a role model?

Christopher Pyne has spat the dummy threatening millions to be cut from research if his tertiary fees proposals aren't passed in the Senate. He looks decidedly unhappy now he can't find the dummy. Poor widdle Cwistohper.

Amazing that Tony has acknowledged Labor's year of ideas because there seems to be none from the government side that fall outside three-word slogans.

It seems the impartiality of the Speaker's role is dead, buried and cremated.

If the government put a tax on any written or verbal criticism aimed against it then it would be in surplus overnight.

Do we hold candlelight vigils for all death row criminals and lodge government protests to the 48% of countries that have it on their books and continue to use it including the US, China, Japan, Iraq, Iran, India, Malaysia and Pakistan? Or does it only matter when Australians are involved?

A guy walks into a doctor's office with a foot firmly planted in his mouth and smelling of onions complaining about leeks in his office.

The doctor thought that was incredible and referred him to a proctologist as he thought the patient was up himself.

Why is Barnaby appearing red faced over the dismissal of his Secretary?

"Good government begins today." There are no Key Performance Indicators. So, it is hard to tell what difference there has been since that statement. To my mind I'm not sure anything has changed. Perhaps we as employers of our MP's should establish KPI's for them.

What was Abbott's book called? "Battlelines". Too many politicians see it as a war game with words. This adversarial type of governing is a waste of time, energy and money. Anyone know of a place where a benevolent dictator is? Must be better than this.

Sadly, the Goons made more sense than the Liberal Party does now. Too many backflips, ministers like MacFarlane not following the script and gaffes from the leader.

Bill Shorten is claimed to have a sneer on his face when asking a question but cast your mind back to the attacks by Abbott on Gillard. It seems that a sneer is something that those in opposition wear s part of their vestments.

All a university degree does is give you a qualification. There is no guarantee of a job and high salary. If unis offered that, then a fee for service would be fair enough. Perhaps the ACCC and consumer affairs should look into whether consumers are being ripped off.

Ever noticed that whenever a minister has to backdown, the PM isn't there to support him/her as that would be guilt by association. Also, there are no nodders in the background and only one flag.

I wonder if the faceless men and women who got Christopher Pyne to backdown have eyebrows?

Even when treated, if Pyne is used for building something that will last more than four years, you have to realise it is just something weak masquerading as something hard.

I thought Christopher scrubbed up well for the presser. A few crumbs of humble pie on his lips and great makeup hid the egg on his face.

"Negotiation is an inexact science." Perhaps we should have a science minister to help Chris out.

Backflip? Political opportunism? Or Pyne just speaking after being told off.

Master chef recipe: Add the bullying tactics of Pyne, Abbott and Nikolic to the metadata collection by Brandis. throw in some prechewed onions and you have an ultra-right-wing government that brooks no dissent. Germany had one of those last century, didn't they?

"When I'm on the rocking chair in 40 years I am hopeful that I'll look back on this and think that in the course of my professional life there may be nothing that was more important." Well said Greg Hunt but based on the Treasurer's aspirational budget, you won't be able to sit back. You will still be working and hoping that the pension start date will kick in before you hit 150.

"The less the internal workings of the Liberal Party are made public, the better off for everybody." that's what happens when metadata gets out and about. Will the Liberal Party's be exempt?

Would have loved to hear Bron say "Balls are not in allowed here!" Two cabinet ministers would remain in the chamber but the collective IQ of the cabinet would only be halved.

Just checked the meaning of fixer - a person who makes arrangements for other people, especially of an illicit or devious kind.

Pyne, the fixer and saviour, has just saved jobs he had promised to cut. Does he slash the seats at the drive-in when he doesn't like the movie too?

Don't need a wide-angle lens to get a shot of all female cabinet ministers.

Tony has offended the Irish, The Indonesians, The Russians, The Chinese and so many others that if all the ambassadors came to express their grievances the cavalcade would be like the opening ceremony march of the nations at the Olympic Games

"MPs have been squirrelled away in their usual sitting week meetings" Does that mean they are all nuts?

Collecting metadata may be a criminal offence.......... stalking.

Prince Harry may be seized as a suspect terrorist. After all he is known as hIS royal highness.

That's all we need, a serving member of the British aristocracy telling us again what to do at Gallipoli.

I have my metadata kept in a cloud. George can find it if he dares. He can look for it in the host nation "Cuckooland"

Opening up super for investing in housing will just drive house prices up. Better to get rid of negative gearing and make the purchase of a house a level playing ground.

Defining a journalist is difficult because profession of journalism has been overwhelmed by commentators rather than journalists. Investigative journalists' reports have been superseded by sound bite comments between ad breaks

Only one good poll for Tony and then so many gaffes and leaks. He had probably thought he had turned back the "votes".

Speaking of collective nouns, what is a collection of metadata called? A millstone? A waste? A privacy issue? An expense?

What about a French connection for the theme for the budget "Liberal, inequality, fraternity (old boys' club)"?

Oh Julie. More metadata gone astray. On St Patrick's day it should be spuds not more leeks!!

So, what happened to the boom of the Howard years? Middle class welfare went rife during those years is now post GFC set to strangle the economy. But that is a sacred cow like negative gearing to all parties.

Our Education minister could do with some maths revision. One bill that is negative when cut in half will be equal two bills in the negative. -a = -b + -b = -2b

Christopher Pyne is the thinking man's court jester. Forget Bruce and Dawe think Abbott and Costello "Who's on First?"

The 2015 National Achievers Conference has been advertised. Not many politicians if any attending I hear.

Perhaps Question Time should be renamed to Questionable Time. There is no eloquence, no substance and just diffidence. And these are our finest debaters?

Abbott has complained about being verballed by Daniel Andrews over the East West Link. Meek, mild Daniel is as gentle as a pussy cat. Perhaps Tony meant furballed?

Tony read the Intergenerational Report. Did he though, read the Australian Human Rights Commission Report as well? Many of his colleagues didn't. Is one more partisan than the other?

Get the Fixer on the job, Joe, so that you can get last year's budget through before this year's one supersedes it.

Christopher Pyne looks like he has just been emasculated..... oh that's right. The Senate did that last night.

The Government can't talk about funding, not because of the upcoming NSW election, but because it is securely wrapped up in red tape.

I'm getting confused. Which side is in Opposition. Joe and Tony are talking about what Labor will do. Have they conceded defeat already?

20 years ago, when you were last a journalist there wasn't metadata to speak of, Tony.

"The Labor Party and the Greens are completely feral. They are obstructing for obstructions' sake," And what a role model he was for them when he was in Opposition.

"I'd rather take a glass half full rather than a glass half empty approach to the achievements of this government when it comes to budget repair." Again, with the drinking Tony. Anyone would think you had a problem apart from Joe, George, Christopher, leadership issues.... I can see why you drink!

Today we saw a debacle not a debate. Every elector should ask where their parliamentarian was at this time. I think that only those who sit in on the entire debate should be allowed to vote. That would fill the house most days.

"We can't afford to stick our heads in the sand and block our ears." but that is the direct action that the Coalition are doing about climate change. They are merely looking for places to sequester carbon, they say.

Perhaps the press should demand that the red tape be removed from Senate photography.

Perhaps pictures of the senate will show just how many bother to turn up to the chamber at all. Small groups maybe all that are there and awake. They would need expensive cardboard cut-outs for photos and there is no budget for that.

The heads of the unis are administrators. Those who now really teach and do research, the true academics, weren't in favour of the changes.

Will Pyne and Abbott now use the defeat of the tertiary education bills to call a double dissolution? It could be a real winner for the Coalition if they do, because Joe won't have to do another unpalatable budget.

The fixer has been fixed (veterinary term) by the Senate

Who amongst us will be game to say anything on this blog if the Senate passes metadata laws? We are not journalists. How many of us will be forced to opt out and then will the Pulse slowly peter out and pass into oblivion in a slow and lingering, painful and not dying with dignity death.

Is there anyone out there with the publishing rights to Tony Abbott's quotable quotes. Probably some Multinational with offices in Ireland, I guess. Shame; Tony's words are very taxing.

Bill Shorten and the Labor Party don't need to do anything. They can just stand back and watch Tony score own goals. Always the team player is our Tony but his actions must be dispiriting for those in his team.

I don't get it. You can say what you like in parliament and then withdraw it and all is right with the world. How feckless are those who represent us!

"Dr Goebbels of economic policy". That is time for the naughty corner, I think.

Malcolm whispers, "Remember the old days when we had just Abbott and Costello to talk about. Now we have the Three Stooges - Chrissie, Joe and Barnaby."

It seems that most politicians are data retentive or should that be something else.

Mr Turnbull is slightly irritated. Perhaps that is because he forgot to check the metadata stored on Wikipedia. "A filibuster is a parliamentary procedure where debate is extended, allowing one or more members to delay or entirely prevent a vote on a given proposal. It is sometimes referred to as talking out a bill or talking a bill to death and characterized as a form of obstruction in a legislature or other decision-making body."

So that means that any further slashing and burning is not required. Joe has got enough out of his last budget.

With the metadata being stored offshore, you can be sure that it will sold on. That's all we need, onions and spam!

I am training my carrier pigeons to withstand torture so as not to reveal their metadata. I don't think they will survive a grilling by George but may taste nice with onion sauce and a Guinness or three.

Joint Parliamentary Committee on "Intelligence and Security" sounds like an oxymoron.

Cory Bernardi's antics are like those in the Pagliacci opera. The opera has an evil clown, a jealous clown and a disloyal clown. All these characterize Cory Bernardi depending on his mood and the situation.

Everything comes in twos these days: a double dissolution, a two-part education bill, Christopher Pyne beside himself when his bills failed, two faced politicians etc. Must be the Noah in them all. The Ark took in animals two by two. But would be that one boat that Tony might not turn back?

Tony Abbott's possible election slogan Free Enterprise At Risk (FEAR). Yes, it will be a FEAR campaign and we will have nothing to fear except FEAR itself.

All this talk of an election and who will win. We already know who won't - the electors.

Just rewriting my CV. I have highlighted my aggressive nature, my lack of tact, my unwillingness to take on other people's ideas and opinions, my inability to think before I speak and my fixation on outmoded ideology. Is there anything else I should put in when I apply for a job as a Prime Minister?

If Bronnie is going to ban all things toxic in the chamber, what policies will the Government have to toss out?

My understanding is that Bob Katter is negotiating with Right Wing Republicans in America to form a new political entity - The Mad Katter's Tea Party.

Mr Abbott: "Labor wouldn't recognise a surplus if they fell on one." I somehow think that any Labor members won't have to worry about that Occ. Health and Safety Issue in the life of the Abbott Government.

Emissions should be a good reason why baked beans should be off the menu at the Pollie Canteen. And Bronnie thought that Dr Laming had brought something toxic into the chamber!

How could Christopher Pyne manage to lean or shake it to the right? Most of us he thought he was as far right as you could go.

Apparently, the man who promoted this government as the infrastructure government is considering a moat to stop boat people. He wants to make Australia an island fortress away from

other nations. The idea was concocted by someone who was a clothes salesman for an emperor somewhere.

What is the best Renewable Energy Target? And what about coal seam gas? What is the use of Question Time when no-one in the Chamber answers the fracking questions?

How could we possibly have a Science Minister? The backward looking of this government would mean we would have a Minister for Alchemy not Science. Joe is trying to turn what once was an economic disaster into not really a problem. Christopher turns poor policy and legislation into whine.

If only we had a Minister for Common-sense we would not need any other ministers or even a PM. Shame that even if the position was created there is no-one at all in Parliament who would be qualified for the job.

Does anyone think that investing in submarines is a bottom of the harbour scheme?

"Our country is safe in a way it wasn't a couple of years ago." That's right. Before we invaded Iraq we were much safer.

Joe's saying to himself as he feels the glare of Julie Bishop, "I must not make eye-contact. I must not make eye-contact. Her eyes have a fatal attraction. Death stare just before my second budget........ I'm glad I didn't reintroduce death duties."

Someone should give Joe some advice. If the Senate doesn't like your economic plan, you will have great difficulty trying to budge it.

So, the sleep deprived politicians can no longer be caught out on camera. How many nodders behind leaders in press conferences are only doing that to avoid actually nodding off to sleep?

To blame previous governments doesn't work. To paraphrase Julie Bishop, "That is so yesterday." The Abbott government was elected on its promises to fix the economy and to so without cuts to education, health, the ABC etc. They have embarked down a path that they didn't apprise the electorate of prior to the election and now have to manage that program of changes through a hostile Senate. These are the choices they have made and need to responsibly deal with it. They have said they will fix it and will be judged accordingly at the next election. Instead of bullying their legislation through they need to negotiate it or won't get anywhere.

You have to ask yourself though, "Does the tail wag the dog or the dog wag the tail?" The spin of the government versus the spin of the press. Have we got a government who is so intent on imposing its will that it will try to crush or outspin the fourth estate.

If Tony wanted to travel quicker around the country why does he use the old RAAF airliners? Surely the high-speed fighter jets we ordered years ago would be perfect. Oh, we haven't got those yet? Surely, we should have bought them from a company that has a pizza place type policy. "If it's not delivered in 3 years, it's free!" Actually, the same pizza place policy should apply to election promises with a slight twist. "If it's not delivered in 3 years, you're out!"

The bank account thing is a nonsense anyway. Dormant accounts can be claimed back from the government if they have been transferred to the Government. What can't be claimed back are the ongoing fees by banks that are charged to dormant accounts that gradually reduce account balances to zero.

Under convention retiring senators are replaced like for like. So expect a white male lawyer. Will the new Senator be as much the same value to Queensland as the retiring one? And if so what does that mean?

What party meeting does a Liberal National Party senator go to. Neither a devout Liberal or a National, does he/she pace the corridors between the two? In Parliament are they two-faced and conflicted about voting for what best suits their constituents. Do they have to have a multiple personality disorder to become a candidate?

A bounce in the polls after onion eating the previous week is too much of a coincidence. Tony is the Machiavelli of Australian politics. Knows his onions does our Tony.

The removal of photographers from the public galleries is the Speaker's ruling. Could that be because some very unflattering shots have been taken? Don't roll your eyes over that suggestion. Barnaby would appear less red-faced and some politicians may prefer that their profile to be more highly regarded.

A politician said that all politicians were liars. He was a liar so that means that all politicians aren't liars. So, if that is the case, was he telling the truth when he said that all politicians are liars. If that is true then............ (an age-old riddle)

If the first Abbott/Hockey budget was really bad and the upcoming one will be boring, what will the one prior to the next election contain if we are still indeed facing a budget emergency? Hopefully treatment for vertigo will soon be on the PBS because of all the spin that is occurring.

Hockey is asleep at the wheel of the barnacle encrusted ship called Titanic that Captain Tony sails?

So, when will politicians ever answer the fracking questions without spin?

Why doesn't Tony fly commercial? There may be too many empty seats on commercial flights if prospective passengers find out Tony's on board.

Julie Bishop was caught "making eyes" at the Treasurer. He best be careful as his job may be on the line if a spill motion is called and the "ayes' have it.

Why isn't Question Time renamed "Wasta Time"?

Please Bill don't quote complex figures at him. Ask him what the deficit is he inherited and what the deficit is now.

Brandis is the latest to do a backflip. Perhaps the past few months have been auditions for he gymnastics team for the next Olympics. All those ageing bodies and the subsequent cost of physiotherapists may cause a strain on the Health Budget.

Dutton is buying a one-way ticket from Nauru to Cambodia for asylum seekers for a mere $40 million dollars. that should help Joe's budget as it will save money as Nauru is expensive. Methinks the holiday accommodation for them in Cambodia won't be as good. More barbed wire, less sanitation. But what does Dutton care? Further out of sight, further out of mind. For asylum seekers it is a case of further out of sight, further out of their minds.

Ex Prime Minister John Howard anoints Tony Abbott as leader. Is Tony really happy with that? I would have preferred to have Malcolm Fraser offering praise if I was Tony. It is infinitely worth more.

Of course, Abbott paid tribute to Morrison and his work done on behalf of women in the service. Without Morrison, Tony would have nothing else to show for his achievements as Minister for Women, except maybe the carbon tax.

With the government's budget ripping the guts out of welfare he may soon be introducing new army chiefs; this time however from the Salvation Army.

Tony has a "a very important state occasion to attend" tomorrow. Bet it is not in the state of NSW as the welcome mat has been withdrawn.

I met a data once and we didn't get on. She asked me for my number and address and now I think she is stalking me!

The same sex marriage bill has been taken off the agenda by the government. I am sure Senator Leyonhjelm is not impressed. He is certainly going to be one very cross bencher. Perhaps the government is no longer trying to win the support of crossbenchers in the Senate or maybe there's the scent of a double dissolution is in the air.

Watched the Goebbels jibe by Abbott again and there was one member behind him in view that was not impressed. My esteem for our Foreign Minister continues to rise.

It would be great if basketball rules were in vogue in Parliament. We could sub out under-performing players although the bench has nothing much to offer on either side. Tony Abbott would have been tech fouled and out of the game long ago. As for time-outs, given how many actually turn up to play on the so few days that the game is played, no-one needs a break really. Traveling would come under greater scrutiny. Players of both teams would be called for offensive and defensive fouls as long as Bronnie wasn't the ref. Christopher Pyne however would still have his shots (bills) rejected when he thought they were guaranteed goals.

It says a lot of the mark of the man that both left-wing and right-wing PM's, party leaders and politicians will be in attendance at Malcolm Fraser's funeral. However, in his post parliamentary days, Malcolm was a man of the people and hopefully they will let everyday people into the ceremony as well.

April

- Pauline Hanson, and George Christensen speak at Reclaim Australia organised far right-wing nationalist rallies in several Australian cities.
- Terrorists kill148 people in Kenya
- An earthquake strikes Nepal and causing 9,018 deaths in Nepal and surrounding countries.
- Australian Human Rights Commission president Gillian Triggs labelled the Federal Government's planned changes to the Racial Discrimination Act as "bad law"

One-term governments allow no long-term planning because an incoming government looks at what the previous government has planned and automatically dismisses it in order to make a point of difference. e.g. in Victoria the scrapping of the Metro Rail link which was set ready to go and was prioritised by Infrastructure Australia. Millions of dollars have been wasted to make a political point. Should we remove major project decisions from childish game-playing politicians at all levels of government?

"A country is judged on how it treats its disadvantaged. We have treated poorly our indigenous people, those seeking asylum and those with a disability over many, many years and little has improved. Now according to all reports, the elderly will be treated harshly because, like the others mentioned, they are seen as not contributing much to society and as a drain on the public purse. Could the same be said of politicians?"

Barack Obama has allowed Americans to open up their hearts and minds to millions of illegal immigrants. In Australia, Scott Morrison and Tony Abbott are busy closing doors even though our "illegals" qualify under UNHCR definitions as refugees. Would Australia be better off with someone with compassion such as

Barack Obama to lead us and help us clean up our environment, enhance our poor global reputation and help us show again the humanity that we were once known for?

Is it time that the "politics" is taken out of governance and only the best ideas of either side are enacted? This might end the extraordinary waste of tax payers' money that occurs when each side tries to hold the other to account. It might lead to clearer long-term objectives, financially sensible decision making and policies that deliver the best outcomes for Australians. Voters might even learn to respect the elected representatives who stop treating politics as a game.

There a perceived raised level of youth violence on the streets in Australia and concern expressed by the community about radicalised youths joining warring factions overseas. The reasons for this be explained by chronic and rising youth unemployment, disengagement of youth because of decline of society's structures such as church, family and organisations, or perhaps the high level of violence in digital games and the lack of understanding that there is no reset button for life.

Just because the framers of our Constitution in the 1890's saw no reason to have a Bill of Rights, isn't it time that Australia adopted one. There are few explicit rights in the Constitution such as the right to vote, trial by jury and freedom of religion. The rest are covered by continual changing legislation, bureaucratic interpretation, or have to be altered by referendum. If we had an effective Bill of Rights, what would be in it?

When burqa, terrorist, ISIL, Iraq and Syria become the buzz words and make the front page, funny how the budget deficit, the Medicare co-payment, global warming, university fees and asylum seekers' mental and physical health disappear off the radar.

A number of large towns have had their major businesses close because of outside influences. How far should governments go to save the jobs of workers within a town? Should they factor in the economic and social issues that arise when mass unemployment hits an area or just let businesses survive on merit alone. Through no fault of their own and weighed down by mortgages, previously fulltime workers are now labelled "leaners" and seen as a burden on society.

"Joy, compassion, honesty, wisdom, philosophy and tolerance are things that can't be bought, sold traded or ultimately survived upon. In today's economics driven society they are seen as having no value at all. But in reality, they are priceless. So why aren't these, the fundamental principles behind any peace process in the Middle East?"

What is the purpose of the statutory body, Infrastructure Australia, when state and federal governments seem to completely ignore its recommendations and instead favour pork barrelling marginal electorates with vote winning projects?

In a time when both major parties state that exemplary leadership is needed, why do politicians show such a poor example of dignity, courtesy and respect for not only each other but for the rest of the community? To say their behaviour is childish is an insult to children.

Is Triggs suffering workplace bullying?

The Federal Government have done it and we shouldn't be surprised. The attack on Gillian Triggs has caused the report into conditions of children in detention to vanish off the radar. Another new crisis comes around and the news of plight of the children is forgotten just as much as they are. Is there a politician somewhere who will stand up for them and continually put pressure on the government until there are none in detention or, are they now, to borrow Julie Bishop's words she used in a different context, "so yesterday"?

May

- Christine Milne resigns as leader of the Australian Greens, and is replaced by Richard Di Natale.
- Tony Abbott announces plans to strip Australian citizenship from dual nationals who go overseas to fight with terrorist groups.
- UK general election results in the first Conservative majority government in 18 years.
- An earthquake again strikes Nepal causing 218 deaths in Nepal and surrounding countries.
- ISIS captures the ancient city of Palmyra in Syria.
- Ireland votes to legalize same-sex marriage, becoming the first country to legalize same-sex marriage by popular vote.

I see Joe has ordered in new laxatives. They are called Under Embargo. He has had difficulty trying to budge it. Just checking to see if they are on the PBS.

Apologies to Bobbie Gentry

It was the 12th of May, another sleepless Canberra night

Hoping most had forgotten, Joe stood up in the press spotlights

Joe had promised a budget that he said would put us all to sleep

This was one promise that the people hoped the government would keep

If the last one had passed it would have caused dreadful carnage

Is it tonight Joseph Benedict Hockey's career becomes beyond salvage?

Apologies to Jimi Hendrix

Hey Joe, where you goin' with cigar in hand

Hey Joe, I said where you goin' with cigar in hand

I'm going to shoot down the PPL

You know I don't mind wrecking anyone else's future plans

I'm going to shoot down the PPL

And be the fiscal terrorist of this fair land

In these terrorist times perhaps some sporting clubs should change their pseudonyms, starting with The Bombers in the AFL

Are you sure that ALL the GST raised is given back to the states and territories? I'm sure that there is postage packing and handling costs and probably a Federal Government tax on the transfer.

We can solve the problem of teenagers making bombs. Bring them some discipline. Reinstitute National Service. That will help............. on second thoughts they will learn how to shoot straight and make better bombs.

The Netflix tax will be merely passed on to consumers. Other Australian based operators are paying GST. Once Netflix does then Australian operators who have been charging a low rate to compete with Netflix will be able to raise their prices. The market will balance out and it will never lose and the consumer will never win. Onya Joe. Competition doesn't drive prices down it just drives expectations of consumers up.

Joe's message to ordinary Australians, "We will seek you out everywhere and take your precious money into our coffers" To big business and multinationals it conveys the message, "You are so big and your fingers are in every pie, so we can't touch you."

With so many backflips by Tony and yet another one on the weekend (PPL) I hope he has good chiropractic cover.

Is George Brandis able to read all our blog entries before they get published or hasn't he finished his speed reading course yet?

How many of our politicians were shortlisted for the one-way trip to Mars on the Mars-One? I nominated so many of them. Sick 'em Marvin!

Good to see Joe is in to waste management. he is reducing expenditure on necessities, reusing old slogans and recycling old unfulfilled promises.

Not kicking goals Joe or as Morrison would have it "a try". It seems that just about everyone is saying "nice try" Joe some with a bit more sarcasm than others. However, the video ref (the Australian Public) have still got the sign up saying "Decision Pending"

So, what sort of person willingly goes into a room with only the budget papers to read and is locked in there? Or was it that boring that journos decided to have a nap time at the company's expense? could someone please tell me if the walls in the lockup room were padded?

When they think the poor don't need cars and that $180,000 is quite common as an annual salary; then you have to worry about their concept of money and the average Australian. In their eyes the notion of a 35+ billion dollar budget deficit is a mere bagatelle, certainly not a crisis or emergency.

I am not sure I understand. This is budget number two for the Abbott government. What happened to the things that didn't get passed in budget number one? Are they in this one too? Do they just keep putting them in until the fine print gets smaller and smaller?

Joe and Tony have just decimated Victoria's share of infrastructure spending. methinks they are not counting on seats in Victoria at the next election. Victorians are getting short-changed in GST, education, health and now infrastructure. Time we had a Victorian PM again.

I am amazed that the Minister for Small Business can talk for the whole of his response time without drawing breath and actually answering the question.

Who writes the Dorothy Dixers? Who decides who will ask them? Like to see some more off the cuff questions.

I know condolence motions are important but the sitting time should be extended for these or they could be at the end. That way they could be a great segue to Joe's budget maudlin speech.

Joe wants to take the bread out of our mouths whilst the Labor caucus get to eat cake.

Hasn't all the good news already been leaked. Joe's budget speech tonight will be full of "you may have heard this on the grapevines and non sequiturs.

Apologies to Stephen Foster and his Swanee River
Unlike what Swannie delivered
On budget day
Hockey thinks he is being clever
Getting the old folks to pay

Congrats to the politicians who have just lost the votes of 80,000 women by calling them fraudulent and rorters.

Does the Speaker get to make up his/her own rules because it seems that way? Bronnie conveniently forgets what props are and aren't. If a quote from Hansard is read out then that should be allowable. The sooner we have an impartial apolitical speaker in place the better.

Ah the money tree! When will the right side of politics acknowledge it was John Howard and Peter Costello who planted and nurtured that noxious weed?

"Have a Go". Coalition can't get beyond three words in their slogan repertoire.

With apologies to Jim Reeves and his song "He'll Have to Go"
While tradies will get new tablets and mobile phones
Retirees will have to sell off their own homes
Education and health have been cut right down to the bone
But all that Joe and Tony can say to us is "Have a go"

The point is that those people with parental leave entitlements as part of their salary package are the ones who are being dudded. They have swapped pay increases for these entitlements and the people who have gained salary increases instead of parental leave entitlements are being rewarded. Not talking about minimum wage. Those who have parental leave entitlements below the cut off level for government parental leave payments are being dudded and there are quite a lot of them particularly in the public service.

There is so much lack of talent or talent being wasted in Parliament. Perhaps we should have a Supercoach team but they wouldn't win many games.

"We are on the threshold of an era of opportunity that our parents could never have dreamed of."

Next, we will hear that no child in Australia will live in poverty.

Or did Joe just omit the word "missed" before opportunity?

Hockey is praising China but the sub building won't go to them, nor even to South Australia. The government should realise that the buying of big boys' toys such as subs, aircraft etc is making a huge hole in the budget. If we cut defence expenditure until we could more afford it then that would be far better than cutting health and education.

Security guards in detention centres have now been given the power to use "reasonable force" if they "reasonably believe" it is necessary to protect life or prevent injury. Has the government lost its reason? Have they forgotten that the same codes of conduct were employed by private security guards in the Abu Ghraib torture and prisoner abuse?

Is anyone willing to have a go in a "Have a Go" sweep to see how many times "Have a Go" is said this week? Please don't have a go at me if you are not interested in having a go.

Research has shown: "The average American attention span in 2013 was about 8 seconds. The average attention span in 2000 was 12 seconds. And then get this kicker - the average attention of a goldfish is 9 seconds." Don't buy American Goldfish!!!!!!!!!!

The Coalition must have done their research and decided that the 80,000 parents being stripped of paid parental leave

entitlements won't cost seats. Hope their electorate profiler doesn't get the sack after the next election.

All those car sales and electrical equipment purchases will be made on imported goods. Yeah that will boost our economy. We have sent manufacturing overseas and this tax break is actually giving foreign aid........... don't tell Joe or he will further cut the foreign aid budget saying that small business cuts are now providing it.

Would you say that the generous salary and perks of being a politician and their superannuation and gold card status on retirement was actually double dipping?

I think Tony is going to Fyshwick but many people will want to "have a go" at him there.

When all the baby boomers become pensioners there may be a different tune being played. It will be called, "Disenfranchise me at Your Peril"

I am a small business owner and if I can claim all the things I buy in the next year or so my business will make a huge loss but I will enjoy the Ferrari and the villa in Tuscany (my overseas office). Thanks Tony and Joe for the no strings attached tax break.

Can we have more funding for the ABC please? Those poor journos in Canberra on Budget night. Expect a frosty tone from them today.

Great call by the Member of Chisholm made a great point about lying and Bronnie was wrong in her response. One side can call another member a liar and be thrown out and the other side gets away with it.

If someone's partner is an asset to a small business and has to leave work to have a baby surely you can write off that asset up to that magical $20000. Just don't call it Paid Parental Leave.

Why is debt seen as a four-letter word?.............. Oh I see!

Tony Abbott still speaks in Parliament as if he is the Opposition Leader. He has the majority in the House but spends more time on berating the Opposition for their taxes, their budget shortfalls,

their lack of governance when actually they are his taxes, his shortfalls and his governance.

Free flu shots in Canberra. So, do politicians line up for a shot in the arm or are they all just pains in the butt?

Let's make up our own special bingo sheet of often used, over used and wrongly used words by politicians. A few suggestions - new paradigm, trust us, adults back in charge, good economic managers, debt crisis, rorting, double dipping, I feel your pain, death cult, mums and dads of Australia, fair go.........

Bill has just seen David Leyonhjelm's bingo sheet and his office is doing a massive rewrite. His speech was reduced to less than two minutes with David Leyonhjelm's intervention.

Budget Reply Speech

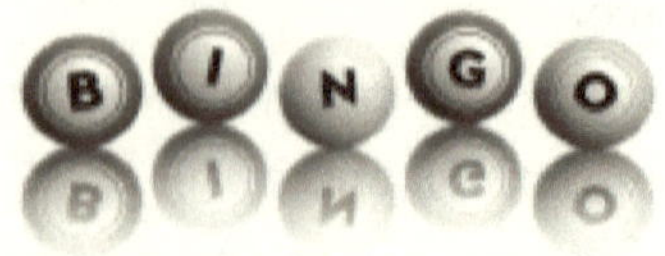

Some lame folksy story about somebody Bill met who told him something	Four-word sentence	"Lets be clear."	Three consecutive sentences starting with the same two words
"Pay their fair share"	"I believe..." [said repeatedly to debunk, once and for all, the suggestion he doesn't believe anything]	"It's about jobs - Tony Abbott's and Joe Hockey's jobs"	More repetition because it worked for Churchill
A $14 billion saving ("like, if you added it up over the next 100 years or something, and include compound interest")	Leave no-one behind	A line by line explanation of what he would do if it was his budget [Just kidding, he won't do that.]	"For all Australians"
Something something about millionaires	Complain about empty slogans, followed by empty slogans	Call for a national summit, because it is time to act	That empty feeling upon realising he didn't actually say anything

Why do we have two sides in politics? The right is never right and the left are often better just left. Wouldn't it be better to have a group of people working for the best interests of Australia and not just for their ideology and themselves............? In the words of Darryl Kerrigan I am sure someone will say "Tell 'im he's dreamin'"

The actual business case for Victoria's East-West link, when it was properly independently analysed showed it to be less than 70 cents in the dollar. In the Napthine released documents the base benefit was 50 cents in the dollar but then they assumed a further 70 cents in the dollar benefit without any real cost analysis see. There was no business case for the entire East-West Link that made economic sense.

Abbott said the Victorian election was a referendum on the EWL and Victorians responded accordingly. To appease Victorians, he said that he would not withdraw the funding but it had to be put to road infrastructure not rail. Now he has done another about face. So, which of the two faces should we believe?

Excuse me, that pre-response may be seen as a premature exclamation.

Hockey has taught us
We are all rorters
Leaners not lifters
And double dippers
Without one zinger
That mudslinger
Shows no empathy
But pleads for sympathy

That's why we have three-year terms of government. Good things will come with a change of government after these three years.

Our current Minister for Women missed the opportunity in the Budget to raise the profile and adequately fund the push against domestic violence.

To encourage people to save for retirement, incentive was given to boost superannuation. This was meant to take pressure off the pension budget bottom line. But those with good superannuation and even better accountants still get the pension. However, what they really want is the pensioner concession card, so perhaps parties should look at providing cards for those over 65 and more thoroughly means test the actual pension money paid. Win for all.

The domestic violence epidemic as it has been labelled is really endemic in our culture. Facts and figures were never reported and are only coming to light. What happened in the home was no-one's business and was not seen as a crime. A verbal and/or physical

assault was put down as a domestic dispute and not what it really was...... an assault.

Turnbull was showing due empathy last night on The Project about domestic violence victims but never really responded to the "Show me the money" questions. Much the same for PPL methinks.

Imagine Barnaby "having a go" at Johnny. In any fight who would come out more red faced?

Johnny Depp will be seen on Border Patrol. What a coup for that TV channel. Hope he gets treated fairly, although fairness is such an overused word these budget days. Obviously, Barnaby has become judge jury and possibly executioner for the dogs.

Let's hope the reply speech by Shorten has had the zingers removed and some passion implanted. One can only hope. If he is full of negativity and no's he will be imitating Abbott's mantra he had when Opposition leader

Let's enlist Shakespeare to help solve the negative gearing issue and politicians double dipping by renting their own/their spouse's house in Canberra. Just rejig his line from Romeo and Juliet to "A tax on both your houses!"

To those who thought Tony Abbott would not be around longer than Mick Malthouse, you have been proven wrong although both have been in charge of a dysfunctional team that as a side has hit rock bottom.

What goes around comes around George. If you are given the power to strip an Australian of their sole citizenship, your turn could be next!

As an ex-school teacher, if a student had referred to another student as "stock" as the Secretary of the Department of Immigration has just done for his fellow human beings, that student would be given detention at the very least!

If Malcolm speaks out radically any more on issues such as marriage, he may be the first victim of the new Minister for Countering Radicalisation and Violent Extremism

Australian politicians love to turn their backs on people. We have been very good at it over the years........ indigenous land rights, stolen generation, paedophilia by the clergy, domestic violence victims and now refugees at sea or in concentration camp type facilities in our "care" in overseas countries. It will be nice to see the backs of some of our politicians after the next election.

I like the join the dots spin of this government. People smuggling is linked to terrorists which means if we accept asylum seekers Australians are supporting terrorism. Next, we will see the earthquake in Nepal being blamed for our cuts in foreign aid........... oh it is.... oops ...sorry!

So, what have we learned? A question is asked. The government diverts, obfuscates, procrastinates, points the finger back at the questioner and then the questioner asks again and the response is similar. It goes on and on. What a waste of time question time is. A chance for two bullying gangs to launch assaults at each other. It is worse than childish and it is such a shame that people have to see that this is how we run our country. Cut the theatrics. The ham acting and sham performance is unworthy of even one star but still the show goes on..........

I'd like to see Morrison's modelling on the "typical" family that he claims earn $100,000 a year and both parents work. They are not in my neighbourhood.

At the State of Origin match tonight, what team will Bronnie be siding with? The ones with blue ties or the ones with red/maroon ones? Impartiality doesn't seem to be her forte.

Heard a great comment by a speaker on ABC 774 Jon Faine's program who said that marriage had nothing to do with love, and that marriage was there as a means of ensuring that procreation occurred. His pro Creationist theory has some strong backing by some politicians. But whether they would publicly say that love has nothing to do with the institution of marriage is another thing............

Domestic violence often leaves the victim emotionally and not just physically abused. Medical certificates can be obtained for each of these results. Victims of domestic violence are often unable to carry out work duties to the best of their abilities after an attack. Would you have them suffer a second penalty such as being sacked for underperforming in the workplace?

Words evolve over a period of time. Customs and human behaviour do too. If not we would be organising marriages as they were in the stone age era. We have had enormous changes in the institution of marriage in the last century alone. Equality between men and women in marriage has changed and is still changing. To place a constraint on the evolution on the meaning of words and to hold to precepts of bygone eras is not the role of one person, but in a democracy, it is of all people. We have elected people to represent us in a vote. Ireland chose to have a referendum instead. Whichever option is chosen we should accept the result whatever it be.

If the next election will be a hygienic election, when the knives come out, will antiseptic will be used?

Regarding the same sex marriage; if you are in a cabinet can you come out of the closet and express an opinion? Is it true that you would then be seen as an outsider like the Irishman Paddy O'Furniture?

Has a muzzle been put on Senator Bernardi? Haven't heard anything from him on the same sex marriage issue.

The 100% tax write off is great for one year as a push. But accountants are warning businesses that if they write $20,000 off this year, those goods can't be depreciated again and so higher taxation will ensue in the following four years. You will pay less tax this year and more tax the following four years. Overall, you end up paying more. Accountants are encouraging businesses to do their sums and read the fine print. One thing for certain is that the government will garner more tax.

So, if Tony is Doctor No, then please someone allocate these bond villains to other appropriate Cabinet members. I can see Joe Hockey as Goldfinger and Scott Morrison as Blofeld.

Tony wants a frank discussion. He will ask the party room to choose between Sinatra and Zappa to be knighted.

Tony has at last realised he can't walk on water. Custard however has different properties and he could on that. However, if he keeps eating profiteroles, he will have to walk off custard.

Did everyone hear Tony mispronounce the word "Hope". When the papers printed what he said there were typos too. Hope, hope hope became nope, nope nope. Fix your hearing aids and spellcheckers please!

At least if there is a conscience vote we will find out if the Coalition members have one. It seems that when it comes to asylum seekers and foreign aid they haven't displayed that they have one yet.

Could someone please tell me how a conscience vote works in Parliament. Does it mean that for other votes they do, politicians have no conscience?

With all the added security at Parliament House how come Julie Bishop's death stare, very much on show today, was permitted to be in the chamber?

This adversarial system of politics is pathetic. We are offered two choices about who is going to run our country and neither in itself is palatable............. sorry about the typo........ it should have said "ruin" not "run"!

The Howard Costello years set us up badly by putting in a middle-class welfare system that neither the Coalition and Labor have the courage to dismantle.

June

- Terrorists kill 220 people in Syria, 38 in Tunisia and 27 in Kuwait on the one day
- Government announces 20-year plan to develop the infrastructure of the north, including transport and water resources.
- Professor Gillian Triggs, chair of the HRC, comes under fire by Peter Dutton for the Human Rights Commission Report on asylum seekers
- China Australia Free Trade Agreement signed
- Joe Hockey said at a time of high unemployment and high house prices, that the starting point for first home buyers is to get a job that pays good money

If a party has established a conscience or free vote for certain pieces of legislation, then what dictates an MP's voting on the remainder of legislation? Is it a collective secret decision of the party room? Is it the researched wishes of the MP's electorate? The MP's own conscience? Would the electorate be happy with the justification "The Whip told me this is how I should vote"?

Why is debate on the bill adjourned? If not enough politicians are in the chamber, then they should send an absence note signed by "Epstein's mother". If it is a regular sitting session, then, if debate is finished by those present, it should be put to the vote.

The Government side looks pretty vacant doesn't it?............. whether there's MP's there or not!

Now is the time for a coup, Bill. No-one is sitting in the coveted seats opposite.

Tony can understand three-word slogans. In this case it is "man and woman". Bill has gone for just two words "two people" so that Tony has some leeway in his thought processing.

How many days do our politicians actually work? There's to be another break. Very few as we've seen today even turn up in the Chamber. Is there a productivity trade-off in their award we could enforce?

How did Bronnie know when to stop the applause without getting the nod from the absent Christopher Pyne?

Terrorists wish to disrupt the everyday life of everyday people in order to assert their power and influence. To continually give them credence promotes their cause. So, getting on with what some see as the mundane is important, lest we all live in fear and in doing so the terrorists have won.

This is the naysayers response to Bill Shorten's new bill. It is to the tune of Paper Lace's "Billy Don't Be a Hero"
"Billy, don't be a hero, don't make the mistake of your life
Billy, don't be a hero, marriage is between man and wife
Billy is just all for show; but at least you're having a go.
Billy, don't be a hero, be like Tony"

Marriage is being gutted by a definitional change that never goes to the people. Abbott is doing the same with another fundamental institution and it is called citizenship.

"Under Mr Morrison's plan a person suspected of terrorism could remain an Australian citizen but lose their right to enter Australia". And that would leave them where? Manus? Nauru?

Now that Abbott is back in Control has Maxwell not so Smart Hockey apologised for the Tampon affair? Or will we never find out because of the Cabinet's cone of Silence.......... (though it never works; hence the leaks last week) Will Siegfried Shorten enlighten us what Kaos will do?

The government and its budget are about small business. Making big businesses small.

Gay and lesbians want a "fair go" too but Abbott and co think those two words apply only to the economy.

To pass a referendum, the bill must ordinarily achieve a double majority: a majority of those voting nationwide, as well as separate majorities in a majority of states (i.e., 4 out of 6 states) The Territories only count towards the National total. That is why a referendum is so hard to pass. You don't need just over 50%. It is more like 66%.

Bronnie has lost all sense of order in the house. It's she who is taking orders from above though.

All's fair in love, war and politics. Well no it isn't. Love - there are no equal rights for gay and lesbians. War - might is right and as such rewrites all history. Politics - just ask the Speaker.

So, our turn back the boats policy has been found out. Today there have been reports of a refugee boat stranded on a reef off an Indonesian island. Our Navy sent them back in a boat they were struggling with at sea only to see them stranded.................. Gotta love Tony's sovereign orders.

How many of our politicians would pass a citizen test by actually honouring what is in the pledge

From this time forward, I pledge my loyalty to Australia and its people, whose democratic beliefs I share,

    whose rights and liberties I respect, and

    whose laws I will uphold and obey.

If Australians were allowed to spend money on what they thought best, then politicians wouldn't get paid.

Think travel and accommodation rorts. Think vote rigging and branch stacking. Think freedom of the press. Think asylum seeker obligations under the UN treaty we signed........................

It seems that you only have to mention the word "terrorist" and you get a bounce in the polls.

Interesting that a bill under debate - the same sex marriage bill wasn't even a topic of conversation in the coalition party room.

perhaps a decision has been made and Tony will inform them how they will vote. Good to see demo.... autocracy at its best.

Has George Christensen spoken to those in his electorate about the SSM bill already? Wow, despite him not being in the chamber when it was introduced, he has been very busy asking for and getting feedback. The marvels of technology.

So, we want to revoke citizenship or ban people returning to Australia, based on the belief that they may have committed treason; without giving them the chance of a judicial hearing, with perhaps any legal challenge being overridden by a politician such as Dutton. Where is the separation of powers?

Under the new citizenship laws that may come to pass, anyone who helped the Irish Catholics in Northern Island would have had their citizenship revoked. Where do you draw the line? As nations we fought against, are now allies? We are fighting with Iran against ISIS yet they were enemies not that long ago. Where are we going to put all those people who have their citizenship revoked? Most state and territory gaols are full. Manus and Nauru would be too severe a form of punishment.

Kevin Andrews seems to be committing us to a war with China. How very generous of him. Strange way to try and take pressure off the housing market?

Early this year it was onions and now it is leeks with Tony. Can we leave the vegie puns please and move on to fruit and nuts for this fruitcake please?

When Bill Shorten introduced the SSM bill most Coalition politicians were absent. Perhaps they were still tucked up in their warm beds dreaming of an unconscious vote.

Surely if does that mean that Mr Abbott was comparing himself to Jesus in his party room parable then he could walk on the water caused by those leaks and rise above it all.

Joe thinks that equity in a home is great but also believes that inequity in so many other things is also very important.

Have just heard a long list of infrastructure proposals and wasn't sure whether I was listening to Question Time or a sound bite from the ABC program "Utopia". Sounded very similar and almost as believable.

I love the camouflage clothing that is the new trend for many members in the chamber. Very effective. Can't see many of them.

Well Captain Tony has just drilled another hole in the Coalition boat to let the water out caused by cabinet leaks. Invoking the Messiah may see him targeted by ultra-orthodox Christians

Global warming is a misnomer. The main concern with greenhouse gases is that they cause major fluctuations in weather events. So, watch out........ coming to a place near you.

"It is a perverse outcome but the erosion of Abbott's singular authority and the reassertion of cabinet decision-making might actually extend Abbott's term by steering him around mistakes he might otherwise make." So, where does that leave Peta Credlin? Is she just the fall person for Abbott's inadequacies?

Tony needed to refer to Moses rather than Jesus and then he could have parted the waters to see where the leak was coming from.

With so much en-light-enment being shown it is a wonder that we aren't encouraging solar power in India. Coal adds CO_2 into the atmosphere. CO_2 leads to major fluctuations in weather conditions including such events as heat waves. It is like opening a fridge to cool a kitchen. The fridge has to work harder and therefore generates more heat and actually warms rather than cools the kitchen.

With all the hot air coming out of Canberra it is only the frosty words from the Speaker and that icy glare from the Minster for Foreign Affairs that keeps any balance.

Tony won't fund rail infrastructure because the whole notion of derailing his budget could leave the Coalition a train wreck.

What I find hard to fathom is that politicians truly believe in their own self-importance and that what they say really matters.

So, let me see. Jesus (Tony) made like Moses (Tony) parted and rejoined the sea (Cabinet) and now has risen like Lazarus and is now trying to pretend not to be like Barabbas who has stolen from the very poor. Heaven forbid that he doesn't get crucified on a poll.

In the House of Representatives just who do the politicians represent? Most people I know aren't belligerent, intolerant or have their noses in the trough. The majority of Australians aren't homophobic misogynists with superiority complexes who belittle others and make fun of them with cheap shots and facile arguments. There is a lot to like about the vast majority of Australians. They work hard, go out of their way to help someone in need, and treat people as they find them without vilifying them because of their race, colour or religious or political affiliation. So, who do those people who sit in the House of Representatives actually represent? Or is the name a misnomer. Should it be renamed the House of Misrepresentation instead?

The definition of an Employment Minister according to Sir Humphrey Appleby is to look after the unemployed. An Education Minister looks after the uneducated and therefore using the same logic a Small Business Minister would be looking after nobody's business.

The government security agency is contemplating installing an enuresis alarm in the Cabinet Room to prevent leaks from p...ed of Ministers.

Impartiality (also called even-handedness or fair-mindedness) is a principle of justice holding that decisions should be based on objective criteria, rather than on the basis of bias, prejudice, or preferring the benefit to one person over another for improper reasons. Antonym - Bronwyn Bishop

Family or domestic violence should be called for what it is; the same as it would be outside a family home. It is rape and assault.

Paedophilia should also be called similarly. Until we use the correct terms, then we are giving a softer countenance to the most serious of crimes.

"We want all Australians to have more money." and the next politician pay rise is all but guaranteed.

Has Kevin Andrews threatened any other country today? Has there been any fallout (hopefully not nuclear) over his belligerent attitude towards flying over the newly made Chinese islands. Look out Dubai you may be on his radar.

People are complaining that politicians are acting like children in the playground. Children in the playground are complaining that they are being likened to politicians.

Bill has just asked for a briefing from relevant authorities so that he can go beyond an in-principle agreement. Tony has denied him that and yet still demands Bill to give a full agreement. Am I seeing circular argument or just Dumb and Dumber

All those leeks in Cabinet are about to be thrown out again. So much for The Think Eat Save Program.

Fourth consecutive drop in living standards. Hockey has just said it was wrong. However, he lies because it is true. So how does Joe get away with it.

Tony's plea, "Stop the leaks or I'll get off this boat and walk home!"

With apologies to Tim Finn and His Six Months in a Leaky Boat

Well it was six months ago
Tumbling down came Abbott's world
Wisdom's suppository, he was all at sea
Seen to be a failure, he was losing all control
The end of his career, Was ever approaching near
He'd be remembered by, all the crap he let fly
He wasn't flash, debonaire,
Had no cold death stare

Abbott's just spent six months in a leaky boat
Lucky just to keep afloat...............

The government can skite all it likes about its improved border security but when it can't keep its own cabinet office secure something is really amiss.

How can politicians get away with lies, half-truths and conjecture? (Tony Abbott regarding wind farm health issues, Peter Dutton's "non-spying" on Sarah Hanson-Young and then calling her a disgrace etc)? We went to Iraq on such speculation about WMD's. Some politicians now deny there was even a GFC. Where is the probity accountability and morality amongst today's politicians? Which face will they show today and just how forked are their tongues?

So which of the following should we believe of Peter Dutton.

"We have not paid people smugglers."

Sarah Hanson-Young was not spied upon and "She makes these allegations which are completely unfounded.."

Gillian Triggs is a "complete disgrace"

If we are to believe him based on these comments, then he is either ill-informed and incompetent or a ruthless politician who dismisses facts and relies on personal attacks. Either way is he the person you want determining citizenship?

Talk about housing affordability. How much does it cost to house the asylum seekers on Nauru and Manus? Now there is one bubble that needs bursting!

In the Great Hall of Parliament House, MPs have gathered to mark the 800th anniversary of the Magna Carta. Yes, there is cake. And so, there should be. Joe's answer to the housing poor affordability was to say "Let them eat cake" John Hewson is still trying to work out if his GST will apply.

The Libs became more in trouble when they promoted Dutton. He botched Health and Sussan Ley has had to come in and fix

up the mistakes. However, the move to Social services has made Morrison move acceptable to the public and perhaps that has been a bad move by Abbott. He now has Turnbull, Bishop and Morrison as far better alternative PM's.

The Same Sex Marriage Bill, Ruddock claims has been politicised, but it needs a change of legislation if it is to proceed. So, it has to be put into a forum where it can be discussed. It is the politicians who put the politics into government. So, if we remove the politicians out of it and just put people who care, are thoughtful ad understand the community, what an improvement in government there would be.

Which one of Tony's Cabinet will lose their citizenship for breaching Cabinet security and thus aiding and abetting the government's enemies (Labor, Greens, Australian Community, Truth and Justice). What a shame that it may be Dutton who has to pass judgement on himself if he was the informant. However, it could be an "I am Spartacus" moment and the whole Cabinet gets voted off the island.

With Apologies to Phoebe Snow and her great song "Poetry Man"
You make us laugh
Though you lie, you think you're right
Such ignominy
Play with your text toy
Or don't listen just read
Trust in your beliefs, yeah, beliefs.
Oh, oh
Don't talk anymore
We don't want to know
You're the Poetry Man
And you waste our time.
"Brandis's reading some poetry, and he don't care where he are."

How many graduates will be waiting tables at the mid-winter politician's ball hoping to earn enough to buy a house, pay off their HECS fee or doing overtime as trainee diplomats?

Operation Sovereign Borders has now got a non-response about the paying of smugglers to turn back boats. The response is that the government won't comment on intelligent matters........... may have to fix my hearing aid.

Why can't we have questions without notice? Speech writers may become unemployed but we will find out just how good a minister actually is. If Dorothy Dixers were outlawed then far more relevant questions could be asked. My local MHR only seems to ask Dorothy Dixers written by someone else and not pertinent to his electorate.

I don't underSTAND Standing orders. To get a seat in Parliament you have to stand. Once elected you have to wait until Parliament sits before you can ask a question which you must stand to ask. You then have to resume your seat according to standing orders. Under other standing orders members are asked to answer questions directly unless they don't understand or misunderstand what has been said by any sitting member........... are you with me so far?............. are you still awake?

So that the person who is currently in the Speaker's or President's chair can better represent their electorate and also to remove any perceived bias of the Speaker of The House of Representatives or by the President of the Senate would each position be better filled by an independent member of the judiciary?

Questions from a political quiz game.

"What is the most important thing for any government to look after."

"National Security"

"What should the general population be the most afraid of?"

"National Security"

What should the general public be not told about?"

"National Security"

"Why are children in detention centres?"

"National Security"

"Why won't you explain whether payment has been made by the government to people smugglers?"

"National Security"

"What have dictators and fascist governments throughout history relied up to keep their position?"

"National Security"

"What are 'On water matters' and why won't you explain what is taking place?"

"National Security"

"Congratulations your answers are 100% correct. For the final question and to become a Minister. What sort of breach was the leaking of Cabinet documents?"

"National Security"

"Superb effort, Minister. Have you anything you would like to add?"

"National Security"

"We have done the right thing, the moral thing, the decent thing, the compassionate thing," Mr Abbott said. Is he mumbling the first lines of his resignation speech?

I wonder how many thought bubbles become policy on non-April Fools Days?

I don't understand why it is so important for politicians to pull each other down to the lowest level. They demean the whole process of government. Let the person who has not sinned cast the first stone. They need to own up to their mistakes and move on so that Australia doesn't waste any more time. They go for a six-week break having done bugger all because their egos get in the way and need to be massaged.

So glad that the Pope has come out saying that global warming is a real issue. Tony now has the papal seal of approval to backflip on his previously held beliefs. Long live the Pope.

I typed ASIO map into Google and clicked on maps and apparently there are no ASIO maps. Do I trust the media, ASIO and Tony Abbott or Google? Thank heavens for Google

Di Natale saying "With each step the government will take us away further away from what is decent" shows how out of step he is in the role of a politician. Government has nothing to do with decency. It has more to do with covering up indecency.

Now it's Andrew Wilkie complaining about inequality. Government has nothing to do with equality. It seems that the decent people who go into parliament don't understand that if they want to become true politicians, they must leave their decency behind and cast aside beliefs of human dignity, equality and altruism.

"The question time walk of shame" is actually the entrance of Bronwyn Bishop.

How can questions be said to be without notice when they have been pre-scripted?

If the Parliament doesn't sit for six weeks can politicians claim the dole? Would that be double dipping if they did? Or with Joe claiming living away from home allowance in his wife's house would that be triple dipping?

Julie Bishop becoming an honorary Matilda should get a 90% pay cut as the Matildas only get 10% of their male soccer counterparts

July

- Tony Abbott and Bill Shorten attend a summit of Aboriginal leaders to discuss a possible 2017 referendum for constitutional recognition of Aboriginal people.
- Royal Commission into family violence begins.
- Greece's debt crisis worsens and it fails to meet an IMF payment. A new government finally agrees to harsher terms.
- Cuba and the United States re-establish full diplomatic relations, ending a 54-year stretch of hostility between the nations.

With the divorce rates so high and lawyers making huge money out of the chaos, some anti-marriage equality proponents should possibly just advocate anti-marriage for everyone.

Don't worry about the free vote, Penny Wong has just been given a free kick by having Cory Bernardi as an opponent. He will be outwitted before the opening remarks. Anyone running a sweep on what part of the debate Cory will use the word bestiality?

It's distraction time everyone! What can we do? We can bomb Syria. We can pretend we are doing something about the current social scourge, "ice". Okay that's covered Friday and today but what can we do tomorrow? And how many more tomorrows until the next election? We will run out of places to bomb and drugs to talk about. We have done the "Coal is good for humanity" We have said wind farms are ugly and cut solar energy subsidies. Think people please! Has anyone got the phone number of the captain of the Tampa?.......

So, what is on the agenda Tony before the next election? You have already announced billions being spent on new ships being built in SA and new subs being built in possibly o..... SA.......ka. What other rabbits have you in your hat? Or is it a one trick Tony we have? Budget's stuffed, so perhaps it will be terrorism and asylum seekers again.

In medieval society a Bishop held a position of might, power and authority, and a Smith was a peasant labourer. How the times have changed but not enough. An Abbott who lacks the understanding of what the common people need, want and deserve is still in charge.

Tony, please do something stupid again. Knight someone, do a captain's pick, offer to shirtfront someone, start a war........ anything; but get our cricket team off the front page. Joe's budget, asylum seekers in detention and parliamentarians' rorting are depressing enough without having our cricket team's efforts greet us in the morning.

There is so much talk about natural disasters being caused by climate change that people have forgotten the disaster that they have created by poor choices at the ballot box. We need a Rational Electoral Target.

Could someone please explain to Senator Bernardi that SSM stands for Same Sex Marriage as he seems to confuse it with BDSM which is Bondage, Discipline, Sadism and Masochism.

With apologies to Monty Python's Galaxy Song from The Meaning of Life

Entitlement rules are laid down, we have found
Perhaps they're not clear enough
Or politicians think we're are stupid or just daft
Perhaps they are just having quite a laugh
What is in and out is all so very confusing
And abusing takes up precious hours
But it's costing us millions every second, we reckon
To keep those we have given all the power
There's rules on perks that're free and subsequent penalties
And every facet that's involved they say
But what is quite a lark, is that up until now

They defend a game they all love to play
So remember, politicians enjoy their sinecure
And we pay them more than they are worth
We pray that there's honest politicians up in space
'Cause there's bugger all down here on Earth

Critics of the global warming concept use ideas like it isn't getting hotter and "coldest winter for 26 years". What they appear to choose to not understand or just plain don't understand is that global warming causes massive fluctuations in weather events. The atmosphere and oceans become out of kilter with what we are used to. So "coldest winter for 26 years" is actually evidence validating global warming.

With the low RET perhaps we will need our ship building industry as the sea levels rise. How many blue-ribbon liberal seats have beach frontages?

Tony Abbott's arguments about the low RET show that he is skating on thin ice and that ice is melting.

In the policy playbook Tony had only three jobs to do. Three slogans of three words each. More than enough for any mere mortal.

He has repealed the Carbon Tax and the Mining Tax

He has stopped the boats.

He has brought the budget back into surplus

.... well two out of three is pretty good. There were no such things as RET and SSM listed so they can be postponed or fobbed off.

Shorten says "I think Mr Abbott just needs to move with the times." He is............ but those times are the 1950's

So, Abbott is actually accidentally writing the Labor Party's next election policy platform. Same sex marriage. Environment. Budget management (because the Libs have just shown they can't do it). University fees. Independence of the ABC............. the list goes on. When the Opposition don't know what position to take,

they ask themselves "What would Tony do?" They then choose the opposite and they know they are on a winner.

I wonder whether Tony will specify that the subs and frigates be coal fired so as to increase our exports? Coal fired subs - surely Tony can see the merit in those.

If the polls keep going in the same direction just watch the deckchairs being hastily rearranged. Is that the orchestra I can here tuning up? I need some ice for my scotch..............a there's some on the starboard side.

So, Tony has the L Plate on. Does that mean: Learner? Leader? Lifter? Leaner? or perhaps Loser? Certainly not small l liberal.

It was a right-wing government who sent us into Vietnam and it was a left-wing government who fought to bring our troops home. The Vietnam War was a waste of human lives and it achieved very little. The veterans, many of room were conscripted, suffered terribly. They were sent because the US believed that the Weapon of Mass Destruction (Communism) would be used against them. We should not have gone but we most definitely should not have treated our troops like pariahs, because they had no choice in the matter. If ever a plebiscite is needed it is for sending our young off as cannon fodder to a war or conflict

How many MP's are worried that come the day after the election they will be unemployed? Given the public attitude to politicians their CV's won't be enhanced by adding "Parliamentarian" on them. Let's see what else we could call it. Hot air dispenser operator? Office mismanager? Trough cleaner? Probably gilding the lily a bit with those though.

August

- Unemployment figures exceed 800,000 for the first time in 20 years
- The Commonwealth Bank of Australia makes a profit of $9.1 billion, a record for an Australian bank.
- Unions Royal Commissioner Dyson Heydon rules that he will not step aside from the Commission over a speaking engagement at a Liberal fundraiser
- A bombing takes place inside a shrine in Bangkok, Thailand, killing 20 people
- Debris found on Réunion Island is confirmed to be that of Malaysia Airlines Flight 370, missing since March 2014
- Several terrorist attacks kill at least 55 in Kabul, Afghanistan.

Glad Broadbent didn't win the speaker's job. He is my local member. Bad enough all he does is ask Dorothy Dixers and nothing pertinent on behalf of our electorate. Imagine him being able to say nothing on behalf of the electorate..... mm little change.

Like in the French Revolution Bronnie has been taken to the scaffold and hoist on her own petard, the blade of the guillotine (chopper) has come down and now Christopher seeks to blame everyone else. Doesn't he realise that it was "a far far unwise thing than she had ever done before"

Is that a brooch Bronnie is wearing or has some humble pie crumb fallen on to her jacket Could it be some left-over egg from her face? What do they serve on first class flights these days?

As a former teacher I was horrified about the rorting of the system by the head honchos in the Victorian Education Department. These people needed to be sacked. As a current voter I am also horrified about the rorting of the system by the members of Parliament. Can we sack these people? Or can they at least put on some extra carriages on the gravy train so that others can get on board.

Tony now must be looking up his "What do I do now?" book. He has hopefully put the Speaker issue behind him. The entitlements rorts will be hosed down as both sides are as guilty as hell. He has announced that he has saved South Australia by turning "on" the boats. Scanning through the pages of the book he appears confused. The first three pages of book were Repeal the Carbon and Mining Tax, Stop the Boats and Bring the Budget to Surplus. Sadly, the rest of his policy play book is filled with blank pages....... now what?

There's a viral YouTube video about a fight between the NFL sides Washington Redskins and Houston Texans. These guys are all wearing helmets and padding!!! It is like question time in Parliament where mock threats and insults are made to try to break through thick skins. It is all theatre, more comedy than drama. Sadly, for all the Australian citizens who appreciate good quality comedy, Parliament is now beyond a joke.

Australia is in dire straits and you appear to be doing nothing........... put the pads on Tony, and play at number four.

George Brandis was supposed to see things only in black and white but he CAN see shades of grey....... perhaps 50... bet that is an image you will see for ever!!!

According to an article in the Melbourne Age, William Shakespeare could well have been on drugs. Most students were willing to take drugs just to try to understand his words or just pass English Lit. So could the Minister of Education and the Minister for the Arts please investigate why students and the masses in general have been subjected to the ravings of a dope fiend.

Bronnie's sour looking demeanour is just because she has taken a pay cut and the Chopper bill has just come in. In line with other employers did Tony just text her to tell her she got the sack?

We have seen two completely different sides of politics today. Warren Entsch showed grace, humility and honour with a simple white rose for the late Don Randall. Bronwyn Bishop refused to applaud the new speaker. Some people have class and dignity. Some don't.

When will some members of Parliament both in the Reps and the Senate finally get it? No-one likes bullies e.g. what Senator Abetz got up to today. No-one likes arrogance e.g. Bronwyn Bishop. No-one likes name-calling e.g. Christophe Pyne. No-one likes the not answering of questions in question time. e.g. Tony Abbott No-one likes snouts in the trough e.g. Tony Burke .... and yet politicians continue to do it. The intellectual and moral ineptitude should cost these people their seats in the next election. If they tried that in the real world as an employer or an employee they'd go out of business or be sacked. Australia's finest don't seem to grace the halls of government these days and we are left with these morally and intellectually bereft cretins............ and what is even sadder is that we elected them.

Sam Dastyari has Mr Bull on his screen. So, does that mean cattle excreta is the "play of the day". Peppa Pig would be so ashamed.

The Renewable Energy Target is irrelevant. According to the Libs we will be invaded by terrorists and all our housing sold to Chinese investors well before 2030. If Labor gets in the Libs have assured us that there will be that many boats arriving that we will be over-run. So, the target is a furphy so they can get elected. It is not a promise and even if it was, then promises are meant to be broken.

"If Coalition MPs are allowed to vote with their conscience it could open the way for same sex marriage to pass federal parliament by the end of the year." That all presupposes that the Coalition MP's have a conscience.

Poor Bronnie, her travel allowance amount only would have got her to the Werribee Sewerage Ponds on her chopper flight and even that would not have passed Joe's sniff test.

I thought local RSL's only ran the old chook raffle. Not saying that Bron is an old chook of course. Still makes the rooster to feather duster analogy quite apt

I thought local RSL's only ran the old chook raffle. Not saying that Bron is an old chook of course. Still makes the rooster to feather duster analogy quite apt

Stuffed African Lion body parts being brought into Australia? What is our new Border Force doing? We won't allow refugees to land but poor old Cecil's bits can make it. The poor old refugees on Manus and Nauru are "stuffed" too.

Many Australians according to the latest opinion polls aren't concerned when Tony Abbott will move into the Lodge but how soon he will move out!

The RET number is what was expected. This might explain the lack of talk. The doomsayers have nothing to say. They are resigned to their fate and are hoping for a change in the political climate at the next election. Those who are climate sceptics know that 26-28% is just a face-saving measure and will achieve nothing except may keep this government elected and to them that is an important thing. Labor and the Greens are rubbing their hands with delight as the environment issue is now theirs to run with and will garner them votes at the next election. The Coalition has paid lip service to the idea. My only concern is for Greg Hunt who now has to explain what he knows is a weak position and one he doesn't believe in.

The Coalition are saying that you can't compare their policy with those of Labor. They need to positively spin theirs not just deride Labor's. Don't they get it. They aren't in Opposition anymore. They are in Government. they are prosecuting their case for a small RET by using a defence strategy. How politically naive they are. They are already trying to shore up a defence that may stop them losing the next election, instead of showing leadership and going out to win the next election. To quote Forrest Gump, "Stupid is as stupid does."

Just checked Master Chef Good Food Guide. Apparently, goat's cheese and Pyne nuts aren't good together.

Tony Smith is losing his first battle. He is not showing impartiality as promised. The bully boys on both sides are pushing boundaries to see how far they can go.... and he is letting them.

Because he doesn't believe he has the numbers in the Liberal Party room to stifle a conscience vote on same sex marriage, Tony has orchestrated a Coalition party room meeting to discuss the conscience vote. Machiavelli could have learned a lot from Tony.

In politics they say all is fair in love and war. But if there is no conscience vote then all is not fair in love. Anything but a conscience vote is unconscionable.

All the hot air currently in the Coalition Party Room should be sequestered into the soil rather than add to the global warming. There is a hole in the ozone layer forming over Canberra.

It seems that the Same Sex Marriage Bill conscience vote and thus the success of the bill itself will be decided in the Coalition Party Room by a predominantly white heterosexual male contingent. And they call it a House of Representatives.

I'm not hedging bets just examining the science. Extreme weather events have always existed. They are now becoming more extreme and more prevalent across wider areas of the globe.

Children have a right to be raised in a safe environment by a loving and caring family of whatever description. Having a mother AND a father doesn't guarantee that. Nor does a same sex marriage or even marriage at all. So, without dismissing your opinion, I merely want to put children's rights into a different context as the right to be raised in a safe environment by a loving and caring family of whatever description supersedes all others.

It is a nonsense that we need a referendum or a plebiscite to change the Marriage Act. John Howard did it without even taking it to an election. He had control of both houses of Parliament and made the alteration to make marriage a union between man and woman. Tony Abbott has made a mockery of the Liberal Party and the party room process by taking it to a Coalition Party Room meeting. The only way that same sex marriage will occur is if members of all parties show some character, some backbone and some confidence. Many have sought advice from their electorate and have said they will back changes. Now they must go against the will of their electorate and probably their own conscience merely to be allowed to hang in with the crowd. These jellyfish may find that their days are numbered and they should make the most of their entitlements while they can. Tony Abbott has just handed yet another winning platform to his opposition. He has given up the green vote and now the rainbow vote. How politically naïve! He may have won the party room battle by devious means but he will find that at the next election he has lost the war.

Entitlements are benefits available to enjoy. After that resounding result at the last election we are entitled to the government we voted for. Perhaps we need a root and branch review of those entitlements.

Team orders be damned. Backbenchers and frontbenchers are elected by voters not by bully boys in party rooms. They should vote on the floor of parliament and not just in the party room. If they truly believe in something the appropriate place to stand up and be counted is the chamber.

How many Coalition MP's will have the courage to cross the floor and sit in the naughty corner?

Frontbenchers, if Tony demands your resignation unless you acquiesce to his demands and go against your principles, what are your principles worth? Don't you know the best way to deal with a bully is to stand up united against one. Ask to be sacked and

see what he does. You are the only thing keeping him in office. Make him realise that. Make your status as a frontbencher worth something.

Abbott was seen as the golden boy years ago. This latter-day Midas has achieved his aim; but whatever he has now touched can be seen for what it is really is........ fool's gold.

A referendum is usually called to change the Constitution. Marriage is not in the Constitution it is laid out as an act of Parliament and that is where it needs to be dealt with.

Someone please tell Tony about the dangers of shooting himself in the foot when it is still in his mouth.

Tony has indicated that heads will roll if his colleagues cross the floor. Now is the time Tony to lead by example!!

It can't be a referendum as it is an act of Parliament that must be changed not the Constitution. A referendum abrogates responsibility and will prove nothing and change nothing.

Entsch said "Even if there was a free vote, there was not enough support in there to be able to support that legislation going through." The problem with that logic is that the whole of parliament was not in that room and if they were, then the public would have a clearer idea if the legislation had enough support and by whom. they would know how their local member/senator voted. Kept in the dark like mushrooms we are and we don't like the taste of the food.

How many degrees of separation from Kevin (Bacon) Rudd is our Tony? Not much. He is running the party room and cabinet like an autocrat.

Someone remind me just how many referendum questions have been resolved in the positive? Abbott's shrewdness has come to the fore. Be it indigenous recognition in the constitution or same sex marriage, the proposals are doomed. Tony Abbott - Master of Cunning Stunts

Some politicians would be better off understanding that their electorate would like them better if they were prepared to cross the floor and not scared to cross their leader.

Liberal MP Dan Tehan wants to send our planes into Syria. In doing so he is metaphorically putting a high vis vest on our defence force in the region who are quietly going about doing their job. Dan Tehan is the son of Marie Tehan who was a Minister in the Victorian Government. Greg Hunt by the way is the son of Alan Hunt who was also a Minister in the Victorian Government. they may not advertise that fact because family is not the in thing at the moment as in the US Jeb Bush (Dubbya's brother) and son of George Bush senior is running for President

The idea of a solar farm is interesting. I understand harvesting energy from the sun but the use of word "farm" sends up all sorts of ideas........... Pigs where the pork crackling is a living thing. Would corn come pre-popped?

And as for wind farms, are they where Heinz get their baked beans from?

Three brave Liberals willing to cross the floor on a point of principle. Robert Menzies would be proud. What he wouldn't be proud of is the way that front and backbenchers are under threat for even contemplating not toeing the line. As conservative as he was, he believed in free speech and the right to hold to principles.

Bill is making himself the smallest target he can at the moment and is stealing the middle ground. Abbott is being exposed for political incompetence by handing Bill ammunition on a daily basis and surrendering the middle ground. The thing is, if Abbott stood strong and firm and started to lead instead of having to put out spotfires of his own creation, the public might view him in a better light and see Bill for what he is.

When politicians arrived after the winter break there was optimism and even a rainbow regarding the same sex marriage

issue. Two days later and the climate has changed. "Snowballs!" was the cry and many agreed that was exactly the Coalition Party showed.

The hardest working person in the government is the spin doctor. However, no matter what he or she does no positive spin is working at the moment. It is like one of those plate twirlers who is frantically trying to stop things crashing down whilst someone (Tony mainly) keeps adding more plates to be twirled.

How Margaret Thatcherish of Tony. When the Iron Lady was in trouble, she contrived the Falkland Wars. Tony is in so much trouble from so many sides he is forced to play the terrorist card and broaden a war. You would never guess who was Prime Minister of Britain when Tony was in Oxford

Careful what you say when using the term et al lest Cory Bernardi see it as referring to halal

Abbott is all at sea over issues such as politician's entitlements, same sex marriage, budget blowouts, the head of the Royal Commission etc. Does that mean he won't comment on "on water" matters?

Abbott has stopped the boats and repealed the carbon tax and mining tax. Job done he has finished what he set out to do. Time to move on. Let someone now take charge who knows something and can actually achieve something.

According to the polls Bill Shorten (BS) is back in vogue. I am not sure when BS went out of fashion when it comes to politics. It can't even be muted on my multimedia devices. I've tried. I have attempted to adjust the balance and it is the same from both sides. From the left speaker you get BS and the same from the right. Perhaps the modern-day models have it built in.

Tony Abbott has been beset by problems out of his control. He didn't cause the issues around politician's entitlements, the Royal Commission Chairman, the desire for some people to be treated equally, the budget problems, global warming etc. He just doesn't know what to say or do. Give the guy a break or he will give up and take up offers to bat at number four for Australia or be the new Essendon coach or Nick Kyrgios's adviser regarding the status of women. These too are impossible and thankless jobs.

The Liberals are in disarray. They are haemorrhaging support. They have internal rumblings. "Whatever it takes" used to be the mantra but that has come at a cost. The person in charge won't accept full responsibility and do the honourable thing and stand down. They don't appear to know what they stand for anymore and there seems that there is no credibility behind their utterances. Constantly being bagged by the press hasn't helped nor has the opposition who can afford to stand back and watch them implode. It seems such a waste of talent. Oops did I say Liberals? I meant Essendon.

Warren Entsch is bringing back the true meaning of being a liberal. A meaning that has been hijacked by others for years. A single white rose one week and huge bouquet of understanding brought to Parliament the next week.

Hardly any Coalition members in the chamber. Are they out getting unemployment cheques or perhaps at Centrelink applying for jobs after the next election?

Marriage doesn't always mean that children are formed from the relationship. There are also laws regarding consanguinity. As far as trendy whims go, throughout history there have been marriages and relationships between same sex couples. It is only recently, in the last two or three hundred years, that we have become prudish about acknowledging the attraction some people have to members of the same gender. So prudish that John Howard changed the marriage act without consultation with the public to make marriage between solely a man and a woman.

I think Warren Entsch's SSM legislation has been "put on ice". Obviously, Tony has gone to the Federal Police to see what to do about a possible drug problem.

Looks like the ACTU is interested in Australia having its own Heydon Collider.

Abbott could be one more opinion poll or one more major stuff up and his colleagues may see that he never gets into the Lodge.

One of the biggest issues that has arisen out of the SSM issue that the Libs have to face is how cabinet and their own party room were manipulated by Tony Abbott. He has effectively told them to toe the line and go against the Liberal party tradition of voting according to their conscience.

Tony Abbott was heard mimicking Sinatra with My Way......... "and now my end is near and my fate seems so uncertain."

So, Abbott was sucking up to a 'Dyson' to get a Rhodes Scholarship.

I

f Sydney MP Ed Husic is sent out for his voluble unhappiness then according to the opinion polls well over half of Australia could be deported.

Question from a member of the Government side: "Could the Minister please improve his handwriting as I can't read the question, he wants me to ask?"

Many of the people representing us from either side don't have much worldly experience.

How many did Bronnie "lose" in her first 5 sitting days in the chair. Or is Smithy just a bit more careless?

Triggs and Heydon - Both of them have been employed to be doing a job without impartiality. Their task is to prepare a report to the government. Labor are doing what the Coalition did and that was to discredit the writer of the report. Both sides are using dishonourable tactics but both parties aren't honourable anyway. The anomaly is that they can be called that in the House of Reps.

Someone, please ask a question of Barnaby. What Tony needs for another week of stuff ups is for Barnaby to go off on day one.

I have question for the Government whip. Where were members of the Coalition when one of your members put forward a private member's bill this morning or is it just important for people to turn up when the cameras are rolling? If a meeting is worthy of Warren's six-hour attendance surely ten minutes of attendance by his colleagues would have been appropriate even if they didn't agree with the proposed bill.

The Libs are in a time warp but it doesn't go back to the Dickensian time period, unless they start using asylum seeker camps as workhouses.

Same recalcitrant got sent out. Speaker from the same side. Parliament should have a truly independent speaker that is not drawn from a political background nor has any links at all with any party. That person should be armed with appropriate punishments for offenders. Name and shame doesn't work. Getting sent out is seen as a badge of courage. Have them clean the toilets at parliament House to see what real work is and what a mess they talk and others have to clean up.

Isn't Canning a highway? So, Tony has to win Canning or it's the highway for him.

Speaking of the Liberal carousel, from the Musical Carousel comes the song "You'll Never Walk Alone". Does that mean one or more of Tony's colleagues will have to push him before he walks?

So, the Cabinet meeting last night couldn't reach a decision about whether to have a plebiscite. Does that mean they will be seeking a community response as to whether there should be a plebiscite? That may take the form of a plebiscite. So a plebiscite to decide on a plebiscite. Could be case of the Russian Doll syndrome. If in doubt they could always ask Putin.

Next captain's call should be "man the lifeboats". I would have said "person" the lifeboats but the Minister for Women has shown with his gender bias towards men in cabinet member selection that it will be "man" the lifeboats and not women and children first. Hope Jules and Sussan can swim.

"Nervous Liberal MPs say that a byelection loss would mean it was 'all over' for Abbott" this was the sub heading in the Age. This means that the people of Canning have had an onerous responsibility thrust upon them. All Australia will be looking at them, many from either side of politics praying for a wise decision. This isn't just an byelection in Canning it may determine the fate of the nation!!!!................ Bit too much hype??? Just trying to emulate the sort of pressure the Coalition and Labor will thrust upon these electors. If Freo and West Coast are playing each other on election day, which team will Bill support and Tony support? You gotta love the timing.

The Senate didn't allow the rebuilding of the Australian Building and Construction Commission. Instead they demolished the government's proposal. There could be evidence presented to the Royal Commission that the government isn't a qualified builder and failed to submit a proper building plan for approval. This could be countered by the government saying the Senate didn't have a demolition order. More headaches for Dyson.

So, Tony read the riot act to the cabinet and warned them not to go off script. He needs better script writers because from where I see things if it was meant to be a comedy it misses lots of opportunities but it is more like a poor soap opera.

"MPs were also asked to leave their mobile phones in another room before they enter the party room meeting" Did that also apply to the Minister for Communications? If he is cast out of the Ministry would that make him the Minister for Excommunications?

Nickolas Varvaris, Luke Howart, Peter Hendy, Karen McNamara, Michelle Landry, Craig Laundy, Rick Wilson, Eric Hutchinson, Nathasha Griggs, David Coleman, Matt Williams, Kevin Hogan, Brett Whiteley, Ann Sudmalis, Fiona Scott, Lucy Wicks, Michael Sukkar, Ross Vasta, Sarah Henderson, Andrew Nikolic, Jason Wood, Teresa Gambaro, Bert van Manen, Louise Markus, Ken Wyatt, Bruce Billson, Warren Entsch, Ewen Jones, Ken O'Dowd, Steve Irons, Peter Dutton, Wyatt Roy, Andrew Southcott, Tony Smith, Luke Simpkins and George Christensen would have lost their seats if the election was held on the weekend according to the polls and Age commentary. Still I am sure that Tony would like the Black Knight see it as just a flesh wound. "Just a couple of Ministers. 'Tis but a scratch. I've had worse. Come on ya pansy."

With James Hird's resignation as Essendon coach there are new employment opportunities in the AFL for any politicians who believe they will be unemployed shortly. Get the job and do lousy at it and you still get a big payout. Sounds the right sort of job for a politician.

Michaelia Cash tried so hard to stay on script. She turned to the policy page and it was blank and the next page was blank and then she... well she just went blank

Spot the difference.

What does George do when people actually use the law to do something, he doesn't want them to do. He changes the law.

What does a schoolyard bully, organising a school yard game, do when the game is not going their way? He or she changes the rules.

And would Gillian Triggs also be a lawyer too? She is also a former professor of law at Melbourne Uni? As President of the Australian Human Rights Commission her position should not have been denigrated either by her integrity being called into question. A pox on both houses.

So JB has become Tony's attack dog today. I wonder whether she is venting anger borne of the terrible situation she finds herself in. As one of the only worthwhile crew members capable of working hard on the SS Titanic, she must wonder about the futility of the course they are on.

"One of the reasons Tony Abbott is such a great leader is because, like the captain or perhaps the coach of the team, he always insists on a team game and he always brings out the best in the players." Tony Abbott - the James Hird of the Coalition. But sadly, no performance enhancing in any way.

I thought cattle excreta was reserved for inside Parliament. Hope Tony doesn't put his foot in it.

Surely "the two-time Sussex Street assassin" is an abusive comment. Has Smithy become just another younger male version of Bronnie. Hope he enjoys helicopter rides and other flights of fantasy.

There are those who say nothing in Question Time and those that say a lot; but even those say nothing.... go figure.

The leaked instruction to spruik that "cabinet is [still] functionally exceptionally well" is really the result of Chinese whispers which began as "That Abbott is dysfunctional as well"

September

- The Australian refugee intake is increased by 12,000 in response to the humanitarian crisis in Syria and Iraq.
- There is a spill of the Liberal Party leadership of the Liberal Party. Tony Abbott is ousted and Malcolm Turnbull becomes PM
- Malcolm Turnbull drops Joe Hockey from the ministry and appoints Scott Morrison as Federal Treasurer
- Federal Government commits $100 million to boost domestic violence services
- A stampede during the Hajj pilgrimage in Mecca kills at least 2,200 people and injures more than 900 others, with more than 650 missing.
- Russia begins air strikes against ISIL and anti-government forces in Syria, to support of the Syrian government

What happens with one term governments? You vote the right one in. You vote the right one out. You put the left one in to shake it all about. They're both a lot of hokey and what have you found? You were right to turf both sides out.

Tony Abbott, when he sees the photo of a dead boy in a policeman's arms, sees a political opportunity. I just see a sad but preventable tragedy. Tony Abbott says, "If you want to stop the deaths, if you want to stop the drownings you have got to stop the boats." How much more would he be lauded if he had said, "If you want to stop the deaths, if you want to stop the drownings you have got to stop the war." Aren't there times when people should recognise that just bombing the crap out of country kills more than it saves?

Many politicians believe that we should go down on our hands and knees and be grateful that they have stood for and now sit in

Parliament. They believe their left or right leanings mirror our own. Whilst they think they are a step ahead or above us, many of us can't stand them..... There's my Pilates done for the day.

Tony Abbott has put restrictions on numbers of asylum seekers from Syria, saying that they are to come out of the overall number of migrant intake so why not more provisos? Will Tony demand that Syrians he will accept be only Christian ones? Or have no allegiance to left wing politics?

Two years of an Abbott government. And good government started when? We know when he said it will start but that was an aspirational goal and we are still waiting. Perhaps it isn't the flames from the celebratory cake's candles that should make the Coalition red faced.

Apparently, Joe has the full backing of his leader. In AFL football terms when a coach is told he has the full support of the board he should register for unemployment. Joe do you know where the nearest Centrelink Office is?

Here's a thought. Instead of dropping millions of dollars of bombs on Syria, drop millions of dollars of aid packages. Instead of spending 55 million dollars on housing four asylum seekers in Cambodia, spend 55 million dollars rehousing all our detained asylum seekers into Australian communities. It may go against policy but hey makes great economic sense.

Threatened Species Day.... and Abbott government celebrates being still intact ..... too much of a coincidence!!

Asylum seekers and refugees aren't endangered species. They are multiplying at an enormous rate. Hopefully this government don't think that bombing the crap out of an area will assist other endangered species.

Have you seen a slo mo replay of politicians speaking? The words seem to still come out at a fast rate but there always a spin on them. Some politicians have an inbuilt echo chamber and the words

are repeated on exit. This is linguistically difficult as many of the speakers have forked tongues.

When Abbott said "Coal was good for humanity.", we didn't understand he had no idea what humanity was. After his reaction to the refugee crisis we now know he still doesn't.

'Mr Ruddock says Australia could take 10,000 people and that would be "a drop in the ocean". If we had taken 10,000 a few weeks ago would have one of the little drops in the ocean have included one now sadly deceased three-year-old?

ISIS have got ready made propaganda. All they have to do is point to the sky and tell people that their enemies are the ones dropping the bombs, killing civilians, destroying infrastructure and homes. But Australia is too smart to fall into that trap. I mean that's what we did in Vietnam, Iraq and Afghanistan. We couldn't be so stupid to do that again could we?.............. oh I see.. we are.

Waffle.............. drivel............ tedium. Will Tony actually answer the question about an extra 10,000 refugees

FTA will become an issue for Labor to deal with. It wants not to block it but refine it. However, the Government spin has it the other way. Bill Shorten needs to strongly articulate the difference. It will be a test of his ability as a leader. Not sure he will get a pass mark though

I wondered when Tony would raise the spectre of a carbon tax again........... welcome back to negative politics 101.

Abbott is like Nero when Rome was burning but hasn't a violin.

The Trump solution may work in Syria - build a wall around it and keep them in there.............. don't tell Tony!!!!

I can't believe I am saying it but Jeff Kennett is right on two fronts. Firstly, we need to open our hearts and borders to those in need. The second part that all it takes is great leadership...................... well that's the hard bit........ can't see anyone with that.

How long does it take to process a refugee? About as long as admitting that we shouldn't have gone into Iraq in 2003.

Apparently, Abbott and Dutton are considering playing Muzak in detention facilities and camps with the occasional interruption saying "Your life is important to us please wait until someone (else) can assist you."

"There will be no requirement for labour market testing to enter into an investment facilitation agreement." that being in the trade deal with China makes a mockery of Government claims. Shorten is right to challenge this one point of the Free Trade Deal or soon even the banana workers (who supply what Australia will have as it's only future sale-able commodity) will also be replaced by overseas workers.

To Paraphrase Leonard Cohen
"Maybe there's a God above
But at last the Libs have learned about love
Not just to bomb somebody and say screw ya
They've been all to ready just to fight
But maybe they've just seen the light
All Australia now thinks Hallelujah
Hallelujah, hallelujah, hallelujah, hallelujah...
Hallelujah, hallelujah, hallelujah, hallelujah...
Hallelujah, hallelujah, hallelujah
Hallelujah, hallelujah"

This is what Abbott does. He wants to balance everything. So, for all the good 12,000 extra refugees will be, he now wants to make more with bombing in Syria. To deter boat people, he punishes those who arrive no matter whether they are refugees or not. He stays in power by agreeing to some extreme right-wing views. Like a tightrope walker he leans one way and then the next but what he stands for/on no-one knows. As a balancer he fails especially on the budget.

If the Canning by-election wasn't just around the corner just how fast and in what way would have the Coalition acted? One wonders whether Tony will discriminate against those refugees who

have arrived in refugee camps in the Middle East and Europe by boat.

"We have a colour-blind policy when it comes to humanitarian support and that will not be changing," so says Christopher Pyne but does that mean that the policy is religious affiliation blind as well?

Cory Bernardi has already decreed that the most vulnerable refugees are "Christians, women, children and families". So, where does he get his information from? Is that UNHCR data? Is it common knowledge on the ground in the camps and in conflict zones? Or does he get it via a direct NBN line from the God he worships?

"Refugees should come to Australia as soon as possible once all the checks have been done." We have a great verification process here. To process an asylum seeker takes years so, to modify an old adage, Don't count the refugees until they've arrived.

I think the insults being thrown around Parliament are terrible. Equating Tony with Baldrick............ Baldrick would be so offended.

If the Black Adder references to Tony continue, come election night we may be able to say, "Alas poor Baldrick, we knew him, Smokin' Jo: a fellow to infinite jest, that no-one did fancy"

Two flag Tony. This indicates the seriousness with which the Libs view the situation............ not very obviously.

If the Refugee intake is to cost $700m. Can we stop bombing and use the money we were spending on destroying infrastructure and homes of refugees to bring more over here. I figure that we will dumping at least $700m worth of ordinance there in the next three months, so that means we could double the refugee intake.

When Tony eventually does die there will be no epitaph as he will be buried at sea. Probably a fitting end as we will all be in boats by then due to global warming and his promotion of it.

On the 7:30 Report Tony shone brightly, gloating in the refugee decision but when asked about the economic situation which has spiralled out of control since he came to power, he blamed the Unions, Labor and the Senate. When he was told that his party was in government, he blamed the ABC for not supporting him. He did say he stopped the boats and repealed the Carbon and mining tax so all is right with the world as that was the plan. He is like one of those dolls with a drawstring in the back that has only a few things programmed in.

Why won't Tony go to Manus island to see for himself what is there? Two reasons. Firstly, he doesn't want to be spied upon and secondly, he is concerned that as he was born overseas, he may find his ticket to Manus Island is stamped one-way like so many others are.

Tony has assured Pacific Leaders that Australia is playing its part on climate change. We add to it so they have something to do rather than sit around and laze on the beach sipping cocktails with umbrellas in them. Meanwhile Tony is singing the Blondie song "The tide is high so I'm moving on....."

Will the refugee situation be Abbott's Tampa moment? Based on public perception, polls and Tony's inability to choose what policies will work and get through the Senate, along with his foot in mouth disease; I think that ship has sailed.

The Coalition should be glad that the Senate voted down having to wait to go onto the dole.......... some will praise it as they line up at Centrelink after the next election.

A red-letter day............... at the stock exchange today. With so much wiped off the value of our best companies, self-funded retirees will be back in the job market, companies will be shedding jobs left right and centre and the 6.2% could represent a low point in our unemployment rate.

Imagine a party that had no affiliations to business or unions. That decided to do what is right for the people it represents. That spent money wisely. That didn't try to politically point score against those that opposed it. That welcomed new ideas. That was prepared to look at long term goals and not at whether it would win the next election.................... oh wait we can't have that. All those current politicians out of work and back in regular society. heaven forbid. we must protect the community. Besides we have the adversarial Westminster system of government here that is anti all those things and promotes division and lauds stupidity.

Just a pipe dream I guess and if it came to pass what would we whinge about?

How can Kevin Andrews say that he is willing to disrespect countries' borders and then complain that asylum seekers are disrespecting ours. Does he have two wigs to sit above both his faces? And of course, it is hard to see the border's dotted lines on the water as they move around a bit. Still ask yourself what Trump would do. Build a wall around a country (worked for East Germany's Berlin). He'd see Australia as having a moat already filled with sharks and crocodiles.

If the Government merely added provisions protecting workers from having their jobs gazumped by foreign workers then the FTA with China would be done and dusted. Both sides are playing political childish games because there is a by-election coming up. Stupid, stupid people running the government and our lives.

I've never understood the background behind the term "pork barrelling". Does it mean that there will be a livestock truck carrying pigs barrelling down the new freeway to be built in the Canning electorate? Must be a coincidence that a decision was made during the by-election campaign, surely.

Peter Dutton, though excused by everyone on the right side of politics, has shown yet another example of his lack of compassion and understanding for those who are doing it tough. Firstly, in the Health portfolio with his attacks on Medicare and co-payments and holding the states to ransom as well as pitting them against each other. Now with his Immigration portfolio he continues his hard as nails attitude to asylum seekers, dismissal of claims of physical and sexual abuse of those in detention and his incredible naivety or contempt about those affected by global warming. He is now being credited with the 12000 refugees being accepted but this government and he were very slow to act and thus one can assume were dragged kicking and screaming into action.

When think about it Peter Dutton's "joke" indicates that Tony Abbott does believe that global warming exists because he laughed.

When you see people grasping on to power at all costs, you wonder whether they have any grasp on reality at all. Never mind the electricity bills, think of what the costs of power are as money is handed out by those wanting to retain or gain power. Again, the public is shafted.

Marginal seat members should always be worried. If they are in fear of losing their seats, they might actually do something. Let's make all seats marginal.

Can the Coalition win with Abbott? Doesn't look possible. The Canning by-election probably won't save him. So, it will come down to timing and who will replace him. A major cabinet reshuffle could happen with a new leader. The key front bench should include regardless of who is prime minister, Turnbull, Bishop (J), Morrison, Ley, Robb, Hunt, Frydenberg, Cash. After that I am struggling. Truss would have to be given a role as leader of the Nationals but it is time that Abbott, Hockey, Joyce, Pyne, Abetz and Brandis stepped aside.

What is with all the press conferences? Surely if something has to be said it should be said in Parliament itself. All this political grandstanding does is cause policy on the run, keep the media employed and the public misinformed. I am so sick of sound bites for the news. Anyone would think that a government could be elected on just three-word slogans................. oh I see.

Will the returning of 2750 gigalitres of water to the river mean that water will stop lapping at the doorway of the Captain's cabin on the SS Dogmatic?

So, when are the Ides of September?

Can Tony manufacture a crisis in time to win the Canning by-election and save his job. Can he invade another country? Visit the troops? Will the flak jacket he wears merely be to defend himself from those within his own party?

Where is a Tampa when he needs one? He couldn't talk about it even then because that would be an "on water" matter. (Even Greg Hunt's announcement about the return of water to the Murray Darling Basin was put to the Immigration Minister.)

Peter Dutton has decided to censor some of the films we used to be able to watch. Predator, Mars Attacks, Alien, War of the Worlds, Men in Black, Close Encounters etc. Apparently, Dutton thinks that alien invasions has something to do with refugees. Even Exodus, Waterworld, Jesus and Life of Pi will be made unavailable as they are "on water matters". Although, The Ten Commandments will be allowed as the water was parted.

An ad campaign for the China Free Trade Agreement? Has it been finalised yet? Has it made it to Parliament yet? I am sick of the China Free-for-all Tirade non-agreement already.

Pyne says if some "choose to retire" then "that opens up opportunities". What a shame he is not the shy and retiring type.

The only boat Tony needs to stop now is the Titanic he now captains............ iceberg ahead!!!!!!

Some people quite rightly are saying, "Where there's smoke, there's fire." However, the issue about leadership has arisen because

of poor policy development and implementation. It has been a case of "where there's smoke, there's mirrors."

"What I think we need is concerted action and maybe a summit might help but what we really want is action," Mr Abbott says. So is Tony channelling Charlton Heston in The Ten Commandments? Tony, the Action Man, again searching for divine inspiration because he has no ideas.

Tony is still acting as if he is in Opposition. He has the numbers to pass any bill (and by-pass Bill) in the House and just needs a couple of votes in the Senate. He is harping on as if it is Labor's fault that he is being obstructed. That is not the case as the hurdles put in his road are of his own design. As a leader he should be forthright and positive. He is not. He is a bully who doesn't like it if anyone stands up to him. He quickly plays the victim then.

Why has it taken so long? Hopefully for the sake of Australian politics and the Australian people that this will be the end of the process and we will have a leader who will move us beyond party politics and create a different, dare I say it, "paradigm".

The Libs have a choice to stay with an unelectable PM or give someone else a chance. Let's see how smart they are.

At least the removal costs for Tony won't have a serious impact on the budget. He never did get to move into the Lodge. One wonders whether Malcolm would see it is a come down to move from Point Piper to Kirribilli.

Shame, The Age is no longer a broadsheet because it now can't fit Julia Gillard's smile in.

What was Malcolm Turnbull silently whistling in the party room when the Abbott contingent including Cory Bernardi arrived? Was it "Send in the Clowns"?

Great display by Bishop junior this morning switching frequently from "It's my party and I'll cry if I want to" to "It's a new dawn, it's a new day, it's a new life and I'm feeling good."

Loved someone's tweet on Q & A saying that as this has been marinading for months, it could be described as a seasoned killing.

Turnbull's challenge speech was brilliant. It said what a lot of Australian's were thinking. Now we need to find out if the words can be matched by the deeds.

We do live in a democracy but we don't vote for a PM, we vote for a local candidate. If that successful candidate belongs to a party that holds a majority in the lower house, then that person can have a say in who will be PM. You can't.

Tony in his last speech as PM tried to rally the troops by saying "We stopped the boats." I think that however for him stopped the votes.

What happens if Tony decides not to hand in his commission to the GG? That would throw a tiger among the pigeons.

In the playground if a bully was challenged and received their comeuppance they would go away and sulk................... just saying.

Nobody knows where poor Tony has gone
Not seen since last night
Is he still holding out hope
That a recount might make things right?
"It's my party, and I'll cry if I want to
Cry if I want to, cry if I want to
You would cry too if it happened to you"
Apologies to Lesley Gore

The Nats have no choice but to stick with the Liberals. They can't cut deals now because an election isn't in the offing just yet. As usual they will kow tow to the more dominant Liberals. There will be a lot of huff and puff but they won't bring the house down.

Christopher Pyne and Julie Bishop seem to be able to pick winners. Julie does it on principles. Christopher doesn't have those but he does have political nous.

Tony could see the GG but not to resign. He could call an election as he is still nominally PM. Wouldn't that be the sign of a drowning man clutching at straws. He obviously didn't take into account the rising tide of public opinion and his life saving skills couldn't save him.

J

ulia Gillard publicly congratulated Kevin Rudd straight after she was ousted and we are still waiting on Tony Abbott to do likewise to Malcolm Turnbull. Says something about the strength of character of both ousted PM's

Tony has always been a man of few words, normally only three, but today he has even reduced that to zero.

Confucius say man who would rather eat onions than chew fat or break bread with others unlikely to turn up to meeting with egg on face and be willing to eat humble pie.

Aliens invading would be perplexed by the response to their question of, "Take me to your leader."

No Tony............ perhaps he has a cunning plan to plot or he can't believe that there was white smoke arising from the party room.

An actual minister for Women. A separate Science Portfolio. And my third wish is ....?

What are the odds on a trifecta for Tony's statement?

1) Stopped the boats

2) Ended the Carbon Tax

3) Got rid of the Mining Tax

I can't believe he has gone. He will be missed. It is so sad for him but his supporters will stay loyal and wish him all the best.............. get better Buddy Franklin

Tony gets to sit next to A Laming who tried to push him off a cliff .... karma.

No one has criticised him for his "decades volunteering at the local surf club or working a shift with the Rural Fire Service" or for

everything else he has done for the community. The criticisms have been about his effectiveness as a PM, his character assassination of Julia Gillard and his inability to articulate his desires in more than three-word slogans. He aspired to the most difficult job in the country and was found wanting when he achieved that. It is a shame that he chose not to wish his successor well and used the word "treachery". Perhaps later on in a time of self-reflection he may realise that he wasn't up to the task of being PM and that there is nothing wrong with that.

Tony received an appropriate gift as he left office. Although many were confiscated at the border. Apparently sour grapes are seen in the same light as Pistol and Boo.

If there is swearing required at the GG's place why is it admonished in the supposed home of free speech, Parliament House?

Question Time has been delayed until 2:30. Answer Time was cancelled years ago.

"I, (insert name here) do swear that I will well and truly serve the people of Australia in the office of Prime Minister and that I will be faithful and bear true allegiance to Her Majesty Queen Elizabeth II, the Queen of Australia, so help me God," So a republican atheist has no chance of becoming a PM

Having to pick a cabinet with some right-wing elements in it may leave Malcolm in a Muddle.

Alas poor Tony (to the tune of I feel the Earth Move by Carole King)

He felt the rug pulled from under his feet
He felt his world tumbling down, crumbling down
To avoid saying lots of dumb things
For hours he went to ground
But maybe he could save face
If he found the right words to say

And take time, to understand them
So he wouldn't leave in disgrace

Tony should have been more worried about the death cult that had emerged in his cabinet and backbench.

Must say Malcolm did okay in QT. He handled the SSM question from Tanya so well. Abbott should take notes in case he gets a recall.

The AFL states dumped Abbott. When an AFL coach dumps its coach, the side invariably wins the next week. What does that say about the Canning by-election or the next Newspoll?

Let all the Mad Hatters like Cory Bernardi, Kevin Andrews and Eric Abetz form their own Tea Party. Even Alice would find them totally strange.

Will we have broken promises or MT promises?

We should we also look at phrenology as a way of determining a person's capacity to perform well. Obviously, we do need a Science Minister to help keep us better informed than the pseudoscience being tossed around as if it were fact.

Will Malcolm have the courage to have any opposition members in his cabinet? What a fantastic step forward it would be for a government and Australia if the best person for the job was chosen regardless of their political affiliation.

Were the tax avoidance changes announced by Mr Hockey today about MP's using their families' houses in Canberra to claim a living away from home allowance?

Can we drop some of the cars Julia Gillard described as old bombs on Syria rather than expensive munitions? Plenty of cheap ones on eBay. I mean there is still a budget emergency isn't there?

Do the people in the electorate of Warringah mind if their current member chooses not to attend parliamentary sittings?

Turnbull has pledged to educate and inform us better. A teacher knows when real education takes place.

A student is taught.

A student remembers.

A student learns and fully understands.

A student applies that understanding.

Abbott, as a teacher, tried rote learning. Simple messages pounded into one's brain. We remembered. We understood how shallow he was and learned to dislike him. We would have applied that understanding at the next election. Hopefully Malcolm has learned from Tony's mistake

People are blaming Julie B and Sco Mo for Tony's demise. Their motive was pure survival. They could see the writing on the wall whilst Tony thought it was just a pretty picture.

Some people say the most uneasy position to hold in a government is now the PM's job. I think the Whip is probably close though.

If Turnbull decided to close Manus Island and Nauru and process asylum seekers expeditiously and fairly on-shore whilst still encouraging people not come by boat, then the economy would be turned around and his rise in the polls would continue exponentially.

Who would have thought that the votes of 54 could change one wavering vote, mine.................... could be thousands of others though.

Will Dutton's career be washed away on an ebbing tide?

To the tune of Sittin' on the Dock of the Bay by Otis Redding

Read it in the Herald Sun

Said that one side had easily won

44 was the losing score

And the winner scored 54

One more Monday game was played

The results were published on Tuesday

The game was up Canberra way

No one knows why

It wasn't played in Victoria

And the G was free that day
But the opponents were barely known
So, no-one really was interested in the game
One more Monday game was played
The results were published on Tuesday
The game was up Canberra way.
No one knows why
Look like nothin's gonna change
Everything, still remains the same
Someone must know what those people really do do
Perhaps someone can explain

October

- Australia and 11 other countries form the Trans-Pacific Partnership
- Malcolm Turnbull announces that the knight and dame classes of honours of the Order of Australia will be abolished
- The Royal Commission into unions clears Bill Shorten of any wrongdoing
- Detainees riot at Christmas Island following the death of an asylum seeker
- A US airstrike on a Médecins Sans Frontières (Doctors Without Borders) hospital in Afghanistan accidentally kills an estimated 20 people
- A series of suicide bombings kills at least 100 people at a peace rally in Ankara, Turkey, and injures more than 400 others.
- Hurricane Patricia becomes the most intense hurricane ever recorded in the Western Hemisphere.
- An earthquake strikes the Hindu Kush region and causes 398 deaths

A joint party room meeting would have seen Tony remain as PM. By that I mean the parties being Liberal, National and Labor. Bill must rueing the day the Libs at last took action. Reminds me of when Fraser decided to call an election early and thought he was up against Bill Hayden only to find out that Bill had been dumped in favour of Bob Hawke.

Tony Abbott lost the job as Liberal leader, promised not to snipe, went AWOL and has come back trying to rewrite history by justifying the job he was doing. However, in saying that policies haven't changed after he was cast aside, he needs to recognise then, that the polling slump he had must then be attributed to his leadership style. Please close your mouth Tony, but remove your foot first.

Has anyone seen the seating plan for the Government side? Will we be playing the game "Where's Tony?" Is that him next to Bronnie? Or will he be one of the bad boys at the back of the classroom next to Joe? It has been a while since he has had a desk in front of him. Will he carve his initials in it? Will there be a white feather rather than a white rose placed in front of his empty seat?

If Tony arrives late will he have a note signed by "Epstein's mother". Will he slink in or make a grand entrance? Has he asked for a seat in the back row so no more knives can be thrust in and people won't see the 54 wounds that are slowly healing although the emotional scarring will take longer?

We need to pay politicians more. Phil Ruddock is reduced to flogging off commemorative mugs. He will probably retire soon and be forced on to a pension. How will he cope. Seriously congrats to Phil. You were a forward-thinking politician when you first arrived and still way ahead of many in your party who have just arrived.

Abbott and Hockey now seated together nearly as far away from the throne as you can get and not within spitting distance of Malcolm. Good move. Spittle and hoiking in Parliament is disgusting and would lower the tone, albeit marginally.

Behind the former prime minister in camera view there was always a cluster of female nodder politicians to give the image that the Liberal Party was inclusive of women. Has that changed?

It seems that Greg Hunt has forgotten to read the paper. He has had extensive discussions with a Matthew Guy and has announced that for Victoria the East-West Link, Metro tunnel and widening the Monash Freeway are infrastructure proposals that the Federal Government would back. Get out of the DeLorean, Mr Hunt. Matthew Guy is no longer the Victorian Planning Minister. The

Liberal/National Party Coalition were turfed out of office a while ago and Tony Abbott's so called "referendum" on the East West Link/ Tunnel was defeated.

If there are no factions in the Liberal Party then how did some ministers retain their portfolios? Every Prime Minister has always had to appease groups within their party to stay in power. The Liberals are no different. The old phrase "keep your friends close but our enemies closer" makes the new seating arrangement for Tony and Joe a big concern.

The "real" Bill Shorten will need to step up to the plate or rather mound. If he can't come up with a better pitch, Turnbull will hit him out of the park at the next election. Perhaps Labor are already looking at elevating their second-string pitcher.

What if Parliament was forced to sit on Saturdays and Sundays? Would politicians see that as an infringement on their working hours and seek penalty rates? At least they wouldn't be attending all the big sporting events trying to be seen and heard.

Are Dorothy Dixer questions a pointless waste of time? Or is that a Dorothy Dixer question in itself?

Can't wait for Tony to ask a Dorothy Dixer. Methinks he will remain very quiet in question time for a long time.

Love the Utopian responses by Truss and Hunt when talking about infrastructure.

Many ministers are so busy that they don't always attend all the parliamentary sittings. So, what will former ministers or Prime Ministers do? For the sake of their electorate will they attend or for the sake of their egos choose not to attend?

Tony has finally learned the pen that the pen is mightier than the sword and his back surgeon has also suggested he keep well away from sharp objects.

Parliament yesterday was like a scene from an old western. A message just had to get through. There was a change in transport

policy as the old one had bogged down and failed to gain traction. Road was not the only way to go. Meanwhile up ahead some people were hoping to derail the process with just a light barricade that they thought that would be enough to bring it to a crashing halt. Greg Hunt stoked the fires with plans to fund Melbourne Metro hidden in among his comments about East-West Link. The warning bells weren't listened to and no-one had an ear to the ground about what was coming. At worst they thought it was light rail and they had the high ground anyway. Shots were fired but a barrage of fire of their own quotes was returned and still the train roared on. This was no old worn out blustering loco as he had been dispensed with. Excess baggage and personnel had also been left at the station. Instead what they faced was a sleek modern engine that had changed tracks. As it smashed through the flimsy opposition, the master engineer, Malcolm, flashed a wry grin as he knew his message had gotten through. Both road and rail would be funded.

Will George also be altering the age that a court recognises that a child becomes an adult?

One of the great things that Tony Abbott did in government was to make Malcolm look so palatable that even Labor voters preferred him over one of his own.

Will we have another stunt played in Parliament where the opposition will be asked to fully back a trade agreement without it having seen the agreement in detail?

Where will Andrew Robb now set his sights? Perhaps with the Philippines as they aren't the in the TPP. We could trade some unwanted refugees for some foreign aid... oh wait that is already in the pipeline

Anyone noticed how quickly Malcolm is moving to tweak policies? Road and rail are now part of the Coalition policy on infrastructure. Attitude of inclusiveness incorporated into discussions about terrorism and religion. Playing down of

economic crisis. Even perhaps some movement on asylum seeker issues.

All are subtle but he is stealing back the middle ground that Abbott had vacated. If he can rein in the rednecks who are advocating harsh policies targeting those who are less able to cope in society, Bill will not be able to demonstrably prove that he offers an alternative government.

If there have been some questionable goings on between the unions and business why are the unions being targeted? Businesses should also be targeted. Shady deals can only take place if there are two or more parties involved. The AWB shady deal with Iraq took two to tango. Isn't that the way it works? Why is business nobody's business?

Irony at its best. No Science minister in the Abbott government and now we have Tony's mentor adding his name to a Science innovation.

Anyone counted how many of the 600 detainees were processed on Nauru that were promised last week? Seems strange that the promise came about the same time as JB was pitching for a greater presence for Australia at the UN. Probably just coincidence.

Do Tony and Joe hang around for rest of the discussions and questions in the chamber after the front benchers leave or is it beneath them?

People should not fear the use of new powers that allow people to be locked up for 28 days, held incommunicado, without trial, without legal representation and without charge. After all would ASIO, George Brandis or Peter Dutton ever make a mistake? And in those 28 days we will only get a glimpse of what asylum seekers have felt and continue to feel for years.

Other countries have done worse; think Gulags and Guantanamo

So, is the economy more important than a fair and just society? Germany in the early 1930's thought so.

Perhaps Malcolm and Lucy could take Charles and Camilla on a tour of Christmas Island, Manus Island and Nauru. That way they could see how global warming and sea level rising will reduce present problems of asylum seeker detention soon.

Australia pays for Royal visits dearly. What is the cost benefit analysis and business case show? After all everything must these days have economic benefit.

The questions need to be asked;

When does personal freedom deserve to be overridden by national security and who decides?

When is it okay for those who expound the notion that justice needs to be blind to all sorts of bigotry, to turn a blind eye and pretend that justice is fair?

If terrorism has caused us to live in fear and institute draconian laws such as the control powers, have the terrorists won?

Phil Ruddock is single-handedly bringing back the budget into surplus...... hope he was able to white out the Made in China labels on the bottoms of the mugs.

Phil Ruddock has just shown what we always thought. "Politics is a mug's game."

Are we surprised that "cross" benchers are unhappy?

Would Tony Abbott have stood in front of The Witches painting instead of witch signs or would have his minders pointed out what was behind him.... although they missed the knife carrying allies.

If all Malcolm Turnbull achieves is to make Bill properly justify why he should be PM and outline the policies he will actually deliver, then Australia will be grateful to Malcolm, because up until now Bill hasn't had to.

Think back. Tony Abbott told Tony Windsor that he would do almost anything to be PM and when he became PM he did almost nothing. Up until now Bill has done nothing to become PM (discounting use of sharp implements).

Can someone please define what welfare is? Is it looking after those who are less well off and on or below the poverty line? When policies dictate there be unemployment should we then further punish those who are unemployed. Do we ignore the disabled and elderly because they are unable to contribute as much in terms of monetary outcomes? Should we rejig the whole system so that people are paid by what they contribute to the system? Business executives would have salaries slashed, teachers and nurses would be paid more but that doesn't help those in the greatest need. It seems that those in the greatest greed get the most and then complain that their moral conscience is being tested if they have to help others.

I wonder whether Peter Dutton could take a leaf out of Tony Abbott's book who as indigenous minister spent a week in Arnhem Land. Perhaps Peter could spend a week in a detention centre on Nauru or Manus Island and get a real feel for his job.

Perhaps Malcolm is considering a new detention centre in the Cayman Islands and will donate it to the cause of keeping asylum seekers off-shore. Strange how he likes to keep assets and asylum seekers both off-shore locked away when he doesn't see asylum seekers as assets.

Will Malcolm also call the bombing of the Medecine sans Frontiere hospital "a shocking, shameful, cowardly crime" and a "deeply personal tragedy" for the victims and their families.

Is it true that Dutton only stayed in the Cabinet because no-one else would take Immigration? Even aspiring secretaries and back-benchers said no thanks.

I've seen volunteers work harder than these people in parliament do. Hell, 7/11 staff work longer hours and are more productive and are below the poverty line. Perhaps the Productivity Commission should investigate Parliamentarians.

With the way AFL player trades are being done today could political parties learn a thing or two? Right wing Labor members of Parliament could be traded for left wing Liberals plus a priority pick in the next draft. Not sure where that leaves "clubs" though that want to offload players that no other club wants. I mean where would a far right wing Liberal or far left wing Labor player go? Probably shouldn't have recruited them in the first place I guess. The political clubs are really so very much alike that wearing a different colour guernsey (tie) wouldn't matter. Wouldn't it be great if we had an All-Australian side chosen and they represented us? Who would be in that side?

At the Flavours of Tasmania shindig were onions or leeks on the menu? Did Tony turn up with egg on his face? Did someone hand him a raw prawn over his attempts to rewrite history? Surely, he wouldn't have tucked into some humble pie if it was available.

Because there are so many leaks from cabinet and party rooms why not televise them and that way there is no confusion about what is being said and by whom. I would like to know how well my rep actually contributes as he appears to do nothing in the chamber. How can I tell if he is representing my electorate properly?

With the Labor Party's ongoing attacks on Malcolm perhaps they should recognise Malcolm is just being "agile" with his money.

"Theoretically everyone could put $1 million into the Cayman Islands. Most people don't have that." Happy for you to put a million in for me Bill. I am happy to supply a brown paper envelope.

Obviously, Tony dilutes his alcohol. That way they become on-water matters and no information is released for security reasons.

Labor don't get it. they have resorted into Tony Abbott like behaviour. When he was in opposition he won because he played the person but when he gained power then we saw how facile he really was. Labor won't win power by targeting a person. One Trick

Tony was a once off. The public won't make the same mistake again. They will respond to better policies. Until Labor is willing to argue on policy not personality they are doomed.

We should forgive Tony for the table. How many tables were broken the night Tony was ousted all around Australia by people dancing for joy.

It seems that everyone wants to move on and put behind Tony's indiscretions and perhaps sweep them under the rug. (We would but for the broken pieces of marble secreted under there.) They should concentrate on more serious matters, like how can a raped refugee's case raise less concerns for Labor and all politicians than a bit of furniture. Just what sort of people have we elected?

As bad as Malcolm may be, Shorten still doesn't sound like a would be Prime Minister in comparison. And Shorten was made to look good by Abbott. So, what does that say about our ex-Prime Minister?

I am happy to bag both sides if they can't see the bleeding obvious. Bill Shorten is like Monty Python's Black Knight and Malcolm is the new King Arthur with his minions (not millions) behind him making appropriate noises when necessary. It would be funny if it didn't involve our taxes and making decisions on our behalf.

Will Social Services Minister Christian Porter please outline the welfare payments that ex politicians get and how they compare with those on low incomes. A simple line graph would be sufficient. Which side of the poverty line would politicians be on?

Remember Joe's advice to would be home owners "First get a good job that pays good money". I wonder how many houses an ambassador to the US can afford? There was no "getting". The job didn't get advertised. There was no application necessary, no key selection criteria, no interviews, no other candidates. There is a difference between getting a job and being given one.

Who in their right mind would give Bill Heffernan a list of suspected paedophiles? Then again, who in their right mind would vote for him as senator?............. I may have just offended the whole state of New South Wales...... please accept my apology and condolences. I was totally unaware that all the fracking had leached brain cell destroying chemicals into the water table.

"I hope you'll be gentle with me," Mr Porter says. "I do bring a very large package." Amazing he can speak with his foot planted in his mouth but at least that way people could check out his shoe size.

How things have suddenly changed since the departure of Abbott. There has been compromise after compromise and workable solutions have been found for China free trade and Social Services legislation for example. Politics is the art of leadership and compromise. Seems Turnbull is an old master and Abbott just drew stick figures.

When a political party issues a "press alert" why aren't the press alert enough to realise that is for the purposes of grandstanding or for distraction. When you want to advertise something issue a press release and when you want to hide something the best way to do it is to call attention to something else.

Nearly question time! Not nearly answer time. With the new rules in play it means that the comedy and theatre will be gone. Nothing of any substance happens in QT, now the ratings will drop too and we will find it out of production............ Thank God. It was beginning to look like repeats of repeats.

The new way to start war. An archduke had to get shot for World War 1 to start. Hitler had to invade Poland for World War 2. Will World War 3 start with an errant emoji?

Does the Medecine sans Frontière hospital accidental loss of life also warrant a full investigation? Or as our ally the US was responsible, so do we sweep it under the carpet?

November

- Four people die in bushfires in Western Australia
- A bushfire kills two people trapped in a car north of Adelaide
- Implementation of a new five-tier terrorism threat advisory system
- Multiple terrorist attacks Paris, France, result in 130 fatalities.

I have a suggestion for tax reform. Means test parliamentary pensions and parliamentary superannuation contributions made by the employer.

I am still unclear as to what constitutes a constituent's question. A relation of Dorothy Dix seems to be living in most electorates.

If this is Bill Shorten's year of ideas so far, we have seen few if any. Does he have no idea? Perhaps there will be a lot released New Year's Eve.

Can you imagine the difference in delivery if Bruce Billson was Immigration Minister rather than Peter Dutton? A happy chirpy game show host instead of a funeral director (with apologies to funeral directors)

It is amazing that assessment of refugees on Christmas Island is still going on yet Minister Dutton has already assessed some as being core criminals. Surely these he should move on.

Follow the logic of politicians if you can.

"We need to grow the economy to be able to offer tax cuts and then people will have more to spend. It will also mean more jobs so more people will have money to spend. People spending more helps grow the economy. But as the economy isn't growing, we have to raise taxes. Raising taxes means the economy can't grow and jobs will be lost. People will not be able to spend and the economy will shrink."

So it comes down simply to revenue versus expenditure and the government reigning in spending as most people have to do when money is tight. The brand-new aircraft on order, do we really need them? And what about the submarines can we postpone those until we find a real naval use for them? Can't we close those extremely expensive to run detention centres in far off places and process people faster and cheaper locally? It is a shame when ideology and common-sense battle and ideology wins out.

Malcolm called Bill, Bill. Tony called him a lot worse and got away with it. You may abuse and humiliate a person but you can't use a first name. Seems almost quaint and human like for a politician to use a first name of a colleague in the chamber. So unlike politicians. So, unlike the way normal people behave. Perhaps Malcolm is trying to fool us into thinking that politicians are normal people too.

Who is playing James Bond in the Coalition and is Spectre the Labor Party? We know that M is overseas on secret business in Indonesia.... Not so secret if you see the posters though.

Does Senator Leyonhjelm realise that he was once a "bundle of dribble and sputum" and that some people still see him as just that?

A bearded man has entered Parliament in an obvious disguise. The clothing isn't "normal" by Australian standards. He is carrying a bag that might contain weapons of mass destruction. But he is let in..... because he says he's Santa. Do you think refugees dressed in Santa costumes would also be freely let in? I mean after all they are heading towards Christmas Island.

I have just tallied up the sitting days of parliament in a calendar year. You know that place where laws are passed. There are more days played by our Australian cricket team. NRL and AFL games are played on more days. Children attend school on more days. This great institution, that determines a lot of how we live and die, how we spend our money and our days and the parameters we coexist by in a society, meets for a very short space of time. There are a lot of unemployed and probably unemployable politicians in Canberra

and they have organised a massive superannuation scheme for themselves in lieu of the dole.

"We have extremist elements at work in this country," Senator Bernardi. Surely that is an extremist point of view.

Some people say that Question Time is just theatre. Given the consistent poor performance by most of the participants, perhaps many Australians would want to get up and walk out. Better still, those there should get up and vacate their seats.

Bill Shorten's new policy on tobacco, "Smoke 'em if you've got 'em but do it now because you won't be able to afford them when we need to balance our budget" could be better and more tactically rephrased as "Quit while you're ahead."

I have a feeling Malcolm will be making a national insecurity statement in reality. We send troops overseas to fight wars because we want to be seen as a big player. We lock up refugees because we fear they will change our life style. We kowtow to all and sundry in our trade agreements. We still have a foreign country's emblem on our flag. Now that is insecurity.

Anyone else think that Shorten is short term?

So, Abbott still thinks that the adage "Let them eat cake" works. No chance of humble pie on his menu but still traces of egg on his face.

I think that Dutton should be careful with the new legislation as it could bite him on the posterior. If it is to prevent "errorists" then he is far more guilty of "errorism" than others. He consistently makes errors in his portfolio, misjudging what is in the best interests for the nation and understanding what the Australian people really want. As an "errorist" he should be sent to 'anus Island

People forget that coal is a renewable energy. It just takes millions of years to renew. Who said that the Libs had no long term vision?

We also have five levels of Prime Minister changeover

not expected, possible, probable, expected, certain

Maths 101.

Cut revenue and spend more equals a negative budget outcome.

Cut revenue and expenditure equals possible balancing of the books although services that are supposed to be provided and are listed as essential are lost.

Increase revenue and maintain expenditure equals perhaps an improvement in budget outcome while services are retained.

Increase revenue and cut expenditure equals election loss

C'mon Sco Mo you do the maths

December

- The Coalition strikes a deal with the Greens to push multi-national tax-avoidance laws through Parliament
- $300 million to be spent on a new strategy aimed at tackling ice drug addiction after a task force review.
- Legislation to allow same-sex couples to adopt passes the Victorian Parliament
- Foreign Minister Julie Bishop is among the signatories to a global climate change agreement after a two-week summit in Paris.
- Scott Morrison delivers the Mid-Year Economic and Fiscal Outlook which predicts a deficit of $37.4 billion for the 2015–16 financial year. Cuts are made in the health and welfare budgets to pay for new spending on immigration, innovation and pharmaceutical subsidies
- At least 116 homes are destroyed by bushfires in Victoria on Christmas Day
- Federal Minister Jamie Briggs resigns his position after admitting being guilty of sexual assault against a female public servant in Hong Kong
- The final report of the Royal Commission unions is released detailing "widespread and deep-seated" misconduct by union officials. Over 40 individuals and organisations are referred to authorities such as the police.
- United Nations Climate Change Conference is held in Paris. A global climate change pact is agreed committing all countries to reduce carbon emissions for the first time

One wonders when Andrew Bolt will enter the political arena and throw his Monty Python Black Knight helmet into the ring to lead the soon to be formed ultra-right wing of the Lib/National

coalition. Here's his climate policy. "climate change....... 'tis but a scratch! Why confuse people with science,,,,,,,,, all those scientists can't all be right....... I will find one who isn't. The Black Knight always triumphs! Have at you! Come on then. Obama against me........... minor flesh wound....... "

All those climate change deniers shouldn't be worried if the sea level rises. After all they probably also believe that the earth is flat and extra water will just fall off the edge.

Regarding the picture of the participants/leaders in the Climate Change Conference I wonder whether one whispered, "If we link arms, we can become a figurative sea wall to combat the rising sea levels." To which another replies, "But would that possibly stop the rising tide of public opinion that says we are doing too little too late?"

Between the climate change sceptics and those who believe it is occurring, the world has polarised. At the same time Polar ice is melting.

So Tony is now saying there was white-anting. He asked for an extra six months and got them. He didn't perform and so was dumped. Any white-anting was self-inflicted and guess what the little termite is doing now to his own party. Hypocrisy at its best. At least Joe only did hip-pocketry.

"Aaaaah!" That's what doctors ask you to say as they push that fat icy-pole stick down your gullet making you almost spew. Well doctors too were almost spewing about Hockey and Abbott's Medicare changes and now they are saying "Aaaaah!" too as Sussan Ley is now pausing discussions. Let's hope it isn't a pregnant pause because obstetric charges are expensive.

Is Malcolm taking a political climate change target to Paris. He hopes to reduce the number of PM changes between now and 2020 by 100%.

Please let us know where politicians are going over the break so that we can avoid them. Seriously though, how many will be taking family overseas with them on important study tours?

Perhaps we should get Cory talk about something he really understands. Okay, contact the Guinness Book of Records people and see what the briefest political speech ever made was.

In this year of ideas, what is so important about a political scalp? Getting rid of Brough won't convince an electorate that you are worth voting for. It's back to the us vs them politics that most Australians hate. Perhaps we should do what has been done with the Holden vs Ford argument; get our politicians made overseas. The ones we have are out-dated and their performance is shite!

Mal Brough looks like he hasn't a leg to stand on. The danger is that he will lose his seat too!!!

When you look at the Ministers that Turnbull has picked you have to wonder about the quality of those who didn't get a gig including Billson, Abetz, Abbott, Hockey etc. Perhaps the Ministry should be reduced so that effectiveness can be improved. Brough and Dutton should be relegated to the outer Ministry or better still outa here. How much deadwood can a cabinet have especially where white-anting is a major risk.

Malcolm, learn from Tony. Look where his uncompromising loyalty to Joe and Peta landed him. Broughy ain't worth it.

Have just changed my mind about wanting to sack Brough. There is no way Cory Bernardi and I think alike!!!

The Australian Characters

- Tony Abbott
- Anthony Albanese
- Cory Bernardi
- Bronwyn Bishop
- Julie Bishop
- George Brandis
- Michaelia Cash
- Mathias Cormann
- Peter Dutton
- Josh Frydenberg
- Julia Gillard
- Pauline Hanson
- Joe Hockey
- Barnaby Joyce
- Craig Kelly
- Jacqui Lambie
- Michael McCormack
- Scott Morrison
- Clive Palmer
- Christopher Pyne
- Kevin Rudd
- Bill Shorten
- Angus Taylor
- Malcolm Turnbull
- Penny Wong

<u>Tony Abbott</u>

Tony Abbott was a very divisive person who rose to Opposition leader after being a minister in an earlier Coalition government. He rose even higher to become Prime Minister. As Opposition leader he was masterful and opposed almost everything that the government put forward. He was also very divisive within his own party ousting Opposition leader Malcolm Turnbull who repaid the favour by ousting him after Abbott became PM. A member of the right wing, Tony Abbott opposed Marriage Equality and Climate Change, denying the later saying that it was 'crap'. He defended big business, refusing to call a Royal Commission into banking and saying that 'Coal was good for humanity'. One of his strangest decisions was to reinstall knighthoods and knight Prince Phillip. After losing the Prime Ministership, he moved to the backbench promising not to undermine and snipe, yet that is precisely what he did and assisted in ousting PM Turnbull. Eventually he was beaten in the 2019 election and his blue-ribbon Liberal seat became an independent one.

<u>Anthony Albanese</u>

A very popular member on the Labor side of politics, Anthony Albanese was narrowly defeated by Bill Shorten as he attempted to become Opposition Leader. After Bill Shorten's defeat in the 2019 election, he was elected Opposition leader. A normally quietly spoken person some believe that he does not have the strength to win an election.

<u>Cory Bernardi</u>

Cory Bernardi as a senator from South Australia for the Liberal Party helped swing the party even further to the right especially on such issues as marriage equality and acceptance of any gender issues including the teaching of sex education in schools. He made the statement that homosexual relationships were just a step away from having sex with animals. A strong fundamentalist Christian he was against abortion and railed against Islam and the immigration of Muslims into Australia and met with ultra-right-wing advocates from overseas. He believed that the ABC as a broadcaster should have its funding reviewed if it continued to express views other than his own. In 2017 just after winning his seat as a Liberal, he split from the Liberal Party to form his own Conservative Party. This party of one eventually failed and he returned to the Liberal fold before announcing his retirement from Parliament in 2020.

<u>Bronwyn Bishop</u>

As Speaker in the House of Representatives who is supposed to be unbiased when making rulings, Bronwyn Bishop ruled with an iron fist and that fist was always on her right hand. The left side, the non-Coalition one, took the brunt of the force she exuded in the position of power she held. She set a record for the number of people she ejected from the chamber. Her position became untenable however because she claimed travel expenses of $5000 for a private helicopter flight to travel 80km to a Liberal party function.

<u>Julie Bishop</u>

Julie Bishop held the deputy leader position for the Liberal government from the time it went into Opposition in 2007 and saw four male colleagues come and go as leader of the party. She was a Minister between 2003 and 2007 and again from 2013 to 2018 when she was Minister for Foreign Affairs. A forthright speaker, she was known for her 'death stare', fashion sense and rarely seen dry sense of humour.

George Brandis

Known as 'Bookshelf Brandis' because of the very large and expensive bookshelves he had installed in his parliamentary office to store all his legal books, George Brandis served as a minister in the dying days of the Howard Government in 2007. From 2013 to 2015 he was made Attorney-General and Minister for the Arts, during which time he cut $105 million from the arts budget. He was left out of the ministry in 2015 but became Leader of the Government in the Senate. He was given a retirement gift of the High Commissionership in London in 2017. He was hailed by all sides of politics for the speech he gave condemning Pauline Hanson's wearing of a burka in the Senate.

<u>Michaelia Cash</u>

Michaelia Cash has seemed out of her depth in whatever portfolios she has been involved in. Accident prone and lacking in the understanding of what her powers are, she has been involved I many gaffes and abuses of power. Prime Ministers have nt known where to hide her. In one case, her staffers did their best and shielded her from questions by the media with a whiteboard. She has beautifully coiffed hair that shows that she is ding her best to delete the ozone layer. As speaker she is very good for the deaf as her lip movements are exaggerated. George H Bush may have said "Read my lips", but with Michaelia Cash, her lips seem to work on their own.

Mathias Cormann

Mathias Cormann held many positions in government and in opposition. His Belgian accent made him sound like Arnold Schwarzenegger but his dry wit and intelligence easily surpassed anything Schwarzenegger had to offer. He was articulate as Leader of the Government in the Senate and often called upon to argue strongly in the public arena on money matters. He served time as Finance Minister and was caught out smoking cigars with Joe Hockey at the time of the budget from hell. When leadership spills occurred as Malcolm Turnbull jockeyed to keep his position, he misread the situation and changed sides which ultimately led to the ascension of Scott Morrison.

Peter Dutton

Unfortunately blessed with the face of a funeral director, Peter Dutton has wielded power in the immigration/home affairs portfolio with the same compassionless façade. His ministry's powers have grown as has his standing within the Liberal Party despite his often poor timed and poor choice of words. He challenged for the leadership against Malcolm Turnbull and on the second challenge felt confident he would win and become PM, only to be undercut by Scott Morrison. A member of the right wing of the government he still manages to steer the government away from a centralist course and often is accused of speaking too much outside his portfolio.

Josh Frydenberg

As a relatively young person Josh Frydenberg moved up the ladder quite quickly to the point where he became deputy leader of the Liberal party and the country's treasurer. His main claim to fame he hopes will be delivering a surplus. However, he should be credited for the work he did to almost secure as Energy Minister an agreement between all parties for an emissions and energy policy. This was ultimately rolled when the right wing of his party forced a spill of leadership and Malcom Turnbull was dumped.

Julia Gillard

Julia Gillard became Australia's first female Prime Minister after Kevin Rudd lost in a leadership spill. She was also one of the most successful ones, managing to pass a lot of legislation despite having a hung parliament and relying on independents to get things through. Her biggest lack of success was in getting an emissions policy through and the scheme that was put forward was blocked by the Opposition who thought it unnecessary and strangely by the Greens who said that it didn't go far enough. Her statement that "there will be no carbon tax under the government I lead" gave the opposition all it needed even though her proposal wasn't a tax at all. It was believed that she was a lame duck going into the next election and a spill saw Kevin Rudd return as PM. She is credited for her beginning the Royal Commission into child abuse which saw many changes in society and ultimately the gaoling of priests and even a cardinal, George Pell. Her misogynism speech in parliament in 2012 aimed directly at Tony Abbott was lauded by women and many men all around the world.

Pauline Hanson

Originally elected to the senate in 1996 as an independent after being earlier taken off the Liberal Party ticket because of her racist views, Pauline Hanson is very right wing and accident prone when it comes to speaking and stunts. She lost her seat, was gaoled and then returned to the senate in 2007, this time not targeting Aborigines and Asians in her maiden speech but instead Muslims. She has been able to manipulate governments as her party One Nation has had balance of power opportunities in the Senate. Her party has had members come and go, some being more outlandish, some finding her views and control too hard to take. Her biggest and strangest stunts, gaffes and speeches have included responding to a question on xenophobia with "Please explain?" indicating she didn't know what it meant; wearing a burka into the senate; having her party associated with the NRA; speaking at ultra-right wing rallies; and releasing a video saying that she had been murdered.

Joe Hockey

Joe Hockey served as a minister in the Howard government from 2001 until 2007 and then became treasurer when the Coalition resumed power in 2013. His handling of the treasury portfolio and the 2014 'horror' budget in particular when he described Australians as 'lifters or leaners' saw him lose his portfolio when Malcolm Turnbull became PM. He retired from parliament only to become Australia's ambassador to the US in what seemed a payoff for services not rendered and also something he was not really qualified to do. Nicknamed "Smokin' Joe" by his enemies after he was caught puffing on a huge cigar with Mathias Cormann, this shadow treasurer who claimed that there was a debt and deficit emergency prior to the 2013 election managed to increase that deficit and debt in his short reign as treasurer.

Barnaby Joyce

He started as a senator in 2005 and in 2013 moved to the Lower House. He was often described as the best retail politician in the Coalition but when he became a minister in 2013 and then leader of the Nationals in 2018, things began to go awry. As a senator he threatened to and did cross the floor but as a cabinet minister he was not supposed to. His maverick persona was dulled. From a rural electorate he was supposed to represent what rural people wanted but that wasn't always the case because he towed the Coalition line. Caught up in the dual citizenship issue he had to recontest his seat and was successful. Best known for his ability to shout, his beetroot red face and his extra marital affair that cost him his position, he was one of those who undermined Malcolm Turnbull.

Craig Kelly

A person with strong right-wing views, Craig Kelly wields a lot of power from the backbench. An avid climate change denier and supporter of coal mining, he speaks out on these issues much to the annoyance of his fellow members of the Coalition. He threatened to join the cross bench if he was challenged for preselection and this bullying tactic worked as he was not challenged and held his seat in the 2019 election.

Jacqui Lambie

Jacqui Lambie is a former defence member and was elected to parliament under the Clive Palmer United Party platform as a senator. Following a fall out with Clive Palmer she became an outspoken independent senator who held the balance of power in the Senate. She had to recontest her seat after being found to have dual citizenship and was successful. She shoots straight and from the hip and horse-trades to get her way on many things.

Michael McCormack

He would rather be known as an important politician than an Elvis impersonator, sadly he is good at neither of those. He was the bland leader needed for the Nationals after the demise of Barnaby Joyce. His vacant look and his boring monotone seem to be a genuine reflection of his personality and his Coalition colleagues and indeed the Opposition as well as many members of the public are genuinely concerned when the PM leaves the country and Michael McCormack is left in charge.

Scott Morrison

In 2018, Scott Morrison seemed surprised when all those around him fell and he became Prime Minister. However, some say that it was heavily planned by his supporters. He set up a masterful campaign, creating himself as the person front and centre, and had few policies to criticise thus he was able to narrowly win the unwinnable election in 2019. Having worked in the tourism industry in New Zealand and Australia where he "left" both these positions before his contract was up, he moved into politics in 2007 and made his way quickly into a shadow ministry position. He became Immigration Minister in 2013 introducing sovereign borders policies and denying the media and public to information on asylum seekers and their detention on Christmas Island, Nauru and Manus Island. In 2014 he was moved to Social Services Minister and then when Malcolm Turnbull became PM, Morrison became Treasurer, a position he held until he became Prime Minister. One Question time in Parliament he brought in a lump of coal as a prop and told the Opposition not to be scared of it. His Pentecostal faith he has raised front and centre and this has left him open to criticism. He made horrendous errors of judgement at the end of 2019 and at the beginning of 2020 when the whole east coast of Australia was hit by bushfires. Taking a holiday to Hawaii at the time seemed to show lack of leadership and even on his return his performance was gaffe ridden. A strong supporter of the coal industry and a climate sceptic, he continues to paint a rosy picture of the country's ability to meet emissions targets. Any criticism of him or any of his colleagues he takes the line of "that's just the Canberra bubble" or he obfuscates, changes the topic, won't answer the question or lies. He has earned the nickname as "Scotty from Marketing" but he much prefers Scomo.

Clive Palmer

Clive Palmer first captured the centre of public attention when as a millionaire with mining interests he decided to splash out on building a full-sized working replica of the Titanic in 2012. Before that he opened a dinosaur theme park with huge models overlooking a golf resort. To *say that the public thought that he was eccentric was an understatement. They thought much less of him when he had cashflow issues with his nickel business, owing massive tax debts, making a whole lot of workers redundant with wages, redundancies and leave owed and at the same time heavily investing in his quest to become a political player in federal parliament through his newly formed Palmer United Party. He achieved success in the latter and had to be taken to court over the former issues where he sought continual delays and then somehow negotiated deals that were very much in his favour. His PUP rose like a phoenix in 2013 and he became a member of the House of Representatives along with four others who became senators but two soon left his party because of his dictatorial approach. By the time the 2016 election came the phoenix was in ashes. It rose again in the 2018 and one sitting senator from Pauline Hanson's One Nation party defected to the UAP. In the 2019 election, under the banner of the United Australia Party, Palmer invested $60 million and succeeded in swaying voters to the conservative side of politics without any of his candidates winning a seat.*

<u>Christopher Pyne</u>

Christopher Pyne came into federal parliament as an MP at the age of 25 in the safe Liberal seat of Sturt. He moved into shadow cabinet in 2008 and when the Coalition came to power in 2013, he became Leader of the House and Minister for Education. He then went on to other ministries before retiring in 2019 having spent 33 years in parliament. He is best known for his dry wit, slightly effeminate voice and for being well liked by all sides of politics. His speed at leaving the chamber when he didn't want to have his vote counted was evident when he and Tony Abbott raced to the doors before they were shut. Christopher proved far too fast for the more athletic Abbott but that was due to his nimble, highly intelligent mind which also left Abbott in its wake.

<u>Kevin Rudd</u>

Kevin Rudd was a Labor leader who had no union affiliations or factions to be beholden to. He had come from the diplomatic corps of the public service and took over as leader of the opposition from the much-liked Kim Beazley in 2006. He took Labor to a landslide win in2007 which saw the sitting Prime Minister, John Howard lose his seat. However, his dictatorial approach to leadership rattled his colleagues and in 2010 Australians woke to find that they had a new PM in Julia Gillard and a new foreign minister in Kevin Rudd. When she looked like facing defeat in 2013 despite having won the 2010 election, she was dumped and Rudd returned as PM in 2013 only to lose the election. Not long after that election Kevin Rudd resigned from parliament. He is best remembered for the apology speech he gave to the indigenous people of Australia and his work in foreign affairs. He remains bitter as to his dumping and regularly adds his voice into the public political discourse.

Bill Shorten

He lost the unlosable election in 2019 because of some very clever campaigning and advertising. As leader of the Opposition for six years until that election he had united the Labor party but hadn't been able to win over the public. His involvement in the removal of Kevin Rudd as PM as well as Julia Gillard as PM didn't help. However, he was a numbers man and had grown up in the union movement and thought he saw the writing on the wall for his party. A Royal Commission into the Union Movement orchestrated by then PM Tony Abbott in an attempt to besmirch Shorten, found no wrongdoing, but it tarnished Shorten's reputation. He is credited with designing the National Disability Insurance Scheme as one of his greatest achievements.

Angus Taylor

The Energy Minister, Angus Taylor has found himself in a lot of hot water. Once seen as future PM material his stocks have fallen low. He has questions to answer on a number of fronts including water buy back schemes where a company he had an interest in made lots of money from the government; doctoring of a document detrimental to the incumbent Sydney Lord Mayor, a position his wife coveted; naming in his maiden speech a well-known author he knew when he was a Rhodes scholar at

Oxford even though she wasn't there at the time; possible unlawful land-clearing on his property. As a strong supporter of coal mining he vigorously defends the government stance on the use/misuse of carbon credits left over from over 20 years before to say that targets will be met.

Malcolm Turnbull

A merchant banker and self-made millionaire, Malcolm Turnbull entered parliament in a blue-ribbon liberal seat and rose through the ranks despite him leading the push for a republic. He played the numbers game after the 2007 election and eventually ousted the newly incumbent leader of the Liberal Party, Brendan Nelson. He was too removed from the job because of his stance on the need for action on climate change, by Tony Abbott. Many years later he would replace Abbot as Prime Minister due to the falling popularity of Abbot. In 2016 he took the government to an election win but was ousted once again because of his climate change stance. He eventually retired from politics and his blue-ribbon seat was taken over by an independent for a short period.

Penny Wong

She is the antithesis of what once was the norm in Australian politics. She is educated, well spoken, surprisingly honest, of Asian extraction and a lesbian. Any of these as well as her gender would see her as the target of political bullying, yet she has risen to Labor's Opposition Leader in the Senate because of her stance over many things including the denigration of women. A strong positive advocate in the Marriage Equality debate, she pulls no punches when she needs to call out bullies, spinners of the truth and outright liars. If she was in the House of Representatives and not the Senate, many believe she would become Australia's second female Prime Minister.

The Overseas Characters

- Jacinda Ardern
- Boris Johnson
- Kim Jong-un
- Theresa May
- Barack Obama
- Xi Jinping
- Vladimir Putin
- The Royal Family
- Donald Trump

Jacinda Ardern

New Zealand's young PM who gave birth while in office, will be remembered for her humanity, stoicism and honesty in really difficult times. She came to world attention after a shooting massacre which ended up with 51 innocent people dying at mosques. Her warmth and sincerity helped heal the country. She was also exceptional when a number of tourists were killed during a volcanic eruption on White Island. Her independence and willingness to speak from the heart at major leadership conferences has been widely acknowledged.

Boris Johnson

Former Lord Mayor of London, Boris Johnson became known as a blond headed fool who sought the limelight, made extravagant promises that he couldn't deliver. Logic said that he was playing well above his capacity and as is the British way, they elected him as PM replacing Theresa May. His rash promises on Brexit and during the election confirming his position may come back to haunt him.

Kim Jong-un

He is the supreme leader of the poor nation of North Korea that has had a succession of leaders all from the one family. Kim Jong-un's rivals from his family seem to mysteriously pass away or disappear. Rather than spend money of feeding the population, Kim Jong-un has spent money on the development of nuclear weapons and ballistic missiles so that he can become a main player on the world stage. He has attracted the attention of China, Japan and the US in particular who have applied trade and other sanctions on North Korea to keep Kim Jong-un in line. Unfortunately, the impact is far more felt on the poor people of North Korea who now have the state-run media telling them that the country is being victimised and oppressed by these countries so North Korea has to fight back. Kim Jong-un seems very artful in wooing attention and exacting promise in return for ones he has no intention of delivering.

Theresa May

May took on the role as PM after the resignation of David Cameron. She had to fight those in her party and those in the Opposition to try to get somewhere in the ongoing saga that was Brexit. Ultimately, she was tossed out by Boris Johnson who said that he had the solution, but has ended up with less than what May had negotiated.

Barack Obama

Spending two terms as president of the US, Barack Obama was the most statesman like president for many years yet it was the downward turning economy that would see his final term being less fruitful. He constantly had to fight battles with the Republican dominated congress and his health care plan that so many poorer Americans would benefit from was a real struggle. In the end a Republican president would dismantle it almost completely.

Xi Jinping

Xi Jinping is the leader of the most highly populated nation in the world and now as President for Life he continues to bring China closer to being the most powerful country in the world. His belt and road policies in poorer countries where he offers infrastructure for influence are getting developing nations on his side. China's expansion into the South China Sea through the creation of artificial islands has caused diplomatic uproar in other nations but Xi Jinping seems unperturbed by that. Rapid expansion has caused difficulties but China is now no longer a developing nation but a major exporter of goods throughout the world. Xi Jinping keeps a close watch over it all and as the companies are largely state run, his leadership decisions are implemented quite quickly and without question. Hong Kong was drawn back into the Chinese control in 1997 and is an essential element of Chinese access to and influence in world trade and affairs. There are major riots occurring in Hong Kong as people are protesting about the crushing of their freedoms. Xi Jinping may be wanting to avoid another Tiananmen Square situation so they haven't been fully crushed as yet.

Vladimir Putin

He took over as President of Russia from Boris Yeltsin in 2000 and through careful swapping of positions with his colleague Dmitry Medvedev (Prime Minister elected in 2000) Putin has led Russia from 2000 through to now. A fitness fanatic and careful diplomat he has improved the circumstances for many of the people in his country whilst still retaining influence in what were states and satellite countries in the old Soviet Union days. Russian military strength is still evident under Putin but also is the use of cyber attacks on countries where Russia now tries to influence election results, most notably the 2016 election in the US. He has often been seen as backing leaderships in countries that are contrary to the ones the US is backing, Syria is a perfect example. This potentially leads to confrontations between the two super powers of Russia and the US and with a diplomatically unstable President Trump in power, the intelligence and guile of Putin in avoiding a conflict has won out so far.

The Royal Family

The royal family began this period with the strange situation where Prince Phillip was given a knighthood by the Australian Prime Minister, Tony Abbott. There have been royal marriages and births as well as scandals involving Prince Andrew and Prince Phillip. The future king's brother, Harry, now married and with a family has asked that he become independent from the throne as another sign that the monarchy is a frail relic that somehow Australia still wishes to cling to.

Donald Trump

Donald Trump was elected president of the United States in 2016 despite his strange behaviour. He defeated Hilary Clinton after bullying and intimidation and a smear campaign. He somehow managed to do the same thing to other Republican candidates and win the candidacy and then the presidency. He has had a high rotation of staff and has put out fake news and uses twitter to state new policies. After seeming to threaten Ukraine with blackmail in order to get information on his own potential opponent he eventually was impeached by the House. He has been continually mocked by world leaders and has met with the president of North Korea among others in what now appears to be a waste of time. He has withdrawn troops from the Middle East leaving the countries there open for more warfare. He has also pulled out of climate change agreements, trade agreements and nuclear agreements. Lacking diplomacy, economic vision and the ability to communicate with women in particular, he has walked the world stage with the world half in fear that the ignorant spoilt brat of a buffoon may one day begin a nuclear war simply because he can.

The issues

- Asylum seekers/Immigration
- Banking
- Border Protection
- Brexit
- Bushfires
- China
- Climate change
- Defence
- Drought
- The economy
- Education
- Elections
- Environment
- First Australians
- Leadership
- Marriage Equality/Gender Equity
- The Media
- Middle East
- North Korea
- Religious Freedoms
- Russia
- Unemployment/Employment
- Unions
- World trade

Asylum seekers/Immigration

Australia has had a major issue with asylum seekers. It has taken over five years before so many of them have been processed. They are incarcerated in concentration type camps in foreign countries including on Nauru and Manus Island. These camps have been funded for by Australia but Australia claims no responsibility. It seems it is an out of sight, out of mind policy that is being enacted. At the end of 2018 moves were afoot to allow asylum seekers trapped in concentration camp type conditions to be assessed by independent doctors and if treatment was needed, they were to be transferred to Australia. This was successful but quickly repealed after the May 2019 election.

Banking

The Australian economy remains reliant on the four-pillar banking system. Four privately owned banks, two of which were once owned by the government, remain dominant and the government seems to be at their beck and call. In the Global Financial Crisis of 2007-2008, the government was forced to underwrite these banks because the banks were so intrinsically part of the economy that if one or more failed the nation would fail. These banks because of their size, power and reach were often seen to be making their own rules. After years of being asked, the Coalition finally called a Royal Commission into the banking sector and the rorts were revealed. However, it seems little has changed.

Border Protection

The Australian government dramatically beefed up its border protection after 2013. Special units of armed "Border Force" personnel were formed and some government departments and spy agencies were melded into one super ministry called Home Affairs with special powers and controlled by one minister, Peter Dutton. Australia had gone from a friendly welcoming place to what some people described as a police state. Freedoms were slowly being eroded, including those of the media.

Brexit

In 2016 There was a referendum in Britain about whether Britain should leave the European Union. The Leave vote was heavily reliant on the push factor of immigration and the loss of jobs and didn't really discuss the consequences of such a departure. The Prime Minister David Cameron resigned when the Brexit result was announced. Theresa May was appointed his replacement and set about working through all the conditions to achieve a Brexit deal and avoid some of the ramifications. In the end it cost her her job and she was replaced with Boris Johnson who called an immediate election to ensure that he had the country's backing. Postponement after postponement had taken place since the referendum but a final date was set when a whole new set of border and economic problems would change Britain forever and perhaps disunite the United Kingdom completely as Northern Ireland and Scotland voted to stay in the European Community.

<u>Bushfires</u>

Australia's climate continues to change for the worse. We have always been a place of 'drought and flooding rain'. After years of drought, massive bushfires hit Australia in the last months of 2019 and the early months of 2020 killing many, destroying homes, livestock, forests and wildlife. Many parts of the whole east coast, parts of Tasmania, South Australia and Western Australia were ablaze and attracted worldwide attention and support. Prime Minister Scott Morrison was loudly and strongly condemned for taking a family holiday during that time and not providing the leadership required. Firefighters, mostly volunteers had not had a break for months because the fires were so severe and were unable to be put out. The navy stepped in and rescued people in isolated towns who had fled to the beaches trying to survive. Months and years before government bodies had asked for more money to buy more equipment but the government had denied their request.

China

China's rise to power as a nation has had major implications on trade with Australia and on its diplomatic defence strategies. It is a major importer of our minerals, especially coal, which China consumes 13% of our exports. We, in turn, import 25% of our goods from China. Australia also provides many opportunities in its universities for Chinese students. Concern has been expressed over the purchase of properties, businesses and opportunities by China in Australia and also China's expansion into the South China Sea. There are also signs that politicians have been influenced by Chinese 'gifts'. Senator Sam Dastyari was forced to resign over his links with Chinese moneylenders. At the moment Australia is caught in the middle of a trade war between the US which sees itself as the leader of the world, and the upwardly moving China that will soon dislodge it. Defence ties with the US and trade ties with China make for awkward negotiations for Australian diplomats and politicians especially as the state-owned Chinese company Huawei wish to become involved in the expansion of Australia's telecommunication network.

Climate change

The vast majority of the population acknowledges that there is global warming caused by increased carbon in the atmosphere and that man through its use of fossil fuels contributes heavily to that carbon. There are people in parliament in Australia who deny such things and are at the beck and call of the mining industry. These same right-wing people have controlled any possible position that the Australian government can take to reduce the emissions. Twice Malcolm Turnbull has lost his position because of it, one when he was Prime Minister. Kevin Rudd and Julia Gillard both lost their Prime Ministerships because of the stance and Tony Abbott rose to power because of it. The Coalition government, with a wafer-thin majority could lose power if some of the ultra conservatives withdraw their support. It is a case of a few controlling the vast majority and Australia and the world suffers because of it.

Defence

Australia relies heavily on the US alliances for defence. This has led us into wars however including Vietnam, two Iraqi wars, Afghanistan and against ISIS. The country spends about 2% GDP on defence. In 2020 this is about $40 billion. Very little equipment is made in Australia and our once great shipyards and other defence industries are just shadows of what they used to be. Major contracts have been signed for submarines and planes that will be delivered many years in the future and possibly by then will be out of date and inferior. For many average Australians who see the photo ops of politicians doing their big boys and their toys routine, the expenditure seems unwarranted and money would be better spent on the homeless, reducing the crippling debt that we have. The military in peace time have done us proud in East Timor and assisting with recovery in disaster situations. They remain independent of the government and the Prime Minister is not the Commander in Chief.

Drought

Australia has been enduring more frequent drought periods of late. They are more widespread, lasting longer and having a bigger impact on the country's ability to grow sustainable crops and to farm traditional livestock. There is a growing belief that the foodbowl that we once were, is becoming a thing of the past. Changing away from traditional methods and recognising that there is a water shortage may help stem the flow of farm foreclosures, farmer suicides and small towns shutting up shops. There are rorts in the Murray Darling water catchment and water allocation. Those downstream suffer the most. Droughts are linked to climate change and the federal government has been slow to act. They are more likely to pout an ambulance at the bottom of a cliff than fence off the top of the cliff.

The economy

Australia has a preoccupation with the economy and that drives policy more than the needs of people. We have ever mounting debt and our GDP has fallen because we rely heavily on mining. Our manufacturing industry has all but stalled. Low wage growth, excessive government spending and poorly funded community service programs like aged pension, unemployment benefits and disability and aged care sectors, mean that the people who need help the most become the first casualties of a stagnant economy.

Education

Australian runs a private and state-run school system. The state-run one is supposed to be free and secular, but that is a matter of debate. By comparison the state-run system is poorly funded compared with the private one as federal government funding flows fairly freely to the private system. This has a real bearing on the social strata that lies under the surface of the egalitarian life that Australians believe they have. Introduction of and publication of testing across schools has not properly assessed student outcomes and instead has set up competition between schools and widened the divide between rich and poor schools both in the private and state-run system. Religious groups such as Catholics run separate schools in the private/independent system and are heavily reliant on federal funding. Come election times, whichever party is in power, school funding is used to benefit the party and its ideology. All schools are *having less time to do their basic work as more and more of society's ills are blamed on the school system and schools are forced to add "fix-ups" into their curriculum.*

Elections

Australians seemed to have a revolving door of Prime Ministers from 2007 onwards. Four times the Prime Ministership was changed without an election. This was very destabilising. After one merry go round ride of Prime Ministers, Tony Abbott swept to power in 2013 only to be part of a domino chain of Prime Ministers leading to Scott Morrison thrust into the position just before an election. He won the unwinnable election by one seat. Many of his counterparts left parliament altogether choosing not to stand rather than lose their seat.

Environment

Australia has a unique environment. It is extremely fragile however and for centuries the indigenous population have managed it. Within the last two centuries since the arrival of Europeans and their land and marine management, there have been massive changes, most of them negative. Entire species of animals have been wiped out and native vegetation has been lost. Heralded all around the world is our Great Barrier Reef but the global warming that has changed the temperature of the water, the use of fertilisers that get washed downstream into the ocean and the introduction of non-native species such as the crown of thorns starfish have decimated a large extent of the reef. Tourism has suffered accordingly. The Reef is a prime example of what is happening across Australia. The Greens political party was set up to provide arguments for a better awareness and management of the environment but they have become just another party, but one of the far left. The public are often left with the feeling of helplessness as the people they elect don't seem to care because the economy is seen to be more important than the environment. Melissa Price was appointed Environment minister by Scott Morrison but had no qualifications apart from a mining background. She made many gaffes and went MIA around election time in 2019.

First Australians

When the Europeans arrived in Australia, they declared the land Terra Nullis indicating that no-one lived there. In doing so, they were stating that the indigenous population were nothing more than fauna, which also meant that the Europeans effectively stole the land from those who had come before them. No treaty such as the one in New Zealand was ever signed. Aborigines became slaves, were conscripted into the army, had their children taken from them to be raised "properly" and were given very few benefits and moved out of productive land. In 1967 they were finally given the right to vote. Under a Labor government in the 1970's they were also allowed to argue for their land rights. For a long period under a conservative government there was little progress made. In 2008 they were finally given a much belated apology about the stolen generation (children taken from their families). In 2017, the celebrated Statement from the Heart was made recommending changes to the way the indigenous population could have a voice about their future. The Coalition government rejected it out of hand.

Leadership

Australia had been devoid of strong leadership since around 1996 in the early days of John Howards prime ministership both in opposition and government at a federal level. The state governments had a number of effective progressive leaders in that time but there was not the quality coming through at a federal level who were willing and capable of leading. Some were trapped in the senate and couldn't become a prime minister. With so many factions in the major parties, would be leaders needed to spend more time unifying their party than unifying the nation. Oppositions and governments were at loggerheads just to prove that there was a point of difference. The image of politicians and indeed leaders went on a downward spiral and may not have bottomed out yet.

Marriage Equality/Gender Equity

The idea that LGBTQI people should be able to legally marry had been the bone of contention for a long long time. Some states wished to make it happen but were wary because the federal government had power to override state laws. It was determined that a law had to be enacted federally to guarantee people the rights that others took for granted. There were all sorts of delaying mechanisms put in place by right wing parliamentarians, media shock jocks and by religious groups. One of these was the introduction of a plebiscite which was a very expensive, non-binding and unnecessary act to slow down the momentum. It was very divisive, yet in the end proved to the politicians that the vast majority of Australians wanted marriage equality to happen. The passing of the law on Marriage Equality was celebrated by LGBTQI and heterosexuals alike and the ultra-conservative politicians when asked to vote in parliament defied their constituents by abstaining or voting no. They proved to be only a minority.

<u>The Media</u>

The media in Australia used to be quite diverse and rules were put in place so that no one person or media company could dominate. However, under changes by the Coalition these rules were relaxed and the Newscorp companies have begun to dominate print, radio and television media, squeezing out the smaller players. The owners of large media companies have extraordinary access to and influence on politicians and policies of parties. Rupert Murdoch is one of the owners who has more say than most. Politicians have been stretching "in confidence" aspects of the law to stop or delay Freedom of Information requests by journalists and when information has been released it has often been heavily redacted. Pressure has been placed on journalists and media groups to reveal sources through the use of Federal Police. Politicians however use the media for the purpose of deliberately leaking of information and have become very fussy whom they will be interviewed by on radio and television. Door stop interviews to create sound bites suitable for the evening news are often held but politicians are finding it difficult to adapt to the 24-hour news cycle and the rise of social media.

Middle East

The Middle East has been a hot bed of uncertainty and division from the earliest of times, some of it religious based, most of it economic. With the rise of the need for oil products, it became and remains a powder keg. At the end of World War 1 artificial lines were drawn on a map separating tribes and families. At the end of the Second World War there was a need to create a Jewish state and the nation of Israel further divided the area. War after war has been fought non-stop between a host of nations. Interference by multinationals and backed by European and US governments has not helped. The ever-present threat of a nuclear holocaust exists and when one renegade Arab group took on the US on US soil causing the 9/11 events, the world held its collective breath. Strategic withdrawal of US European and Russian troops seems unlikely as this led to the rise of other groups such as Al-Qaeda and ISIS. Underlying all this is the world's need for petroleum-based products.

North Korea

This poor impoverished reclusive nation has been under the rule of one family since 1948. Money is spent on developing nuclear capabilities and missiles to strike countries. Surrounded by China, Russia and South Korea, its leaders have been able to get the population to believe that they are under imminent attack. Widely seen as a renegade state, it manages to strut a high profile and threaten countries around it.

Religious Freedoms

Australia has a good set of discrimination laws despite it not actually having a bill of rights. After the religious community were rolled in the Marriage Equality discussion, plebiscite and vote, voices were raised about enshrining discriminatory rights for religions into law. Australia is supposed to have a separation between church and state, through secular governments. This is more in name than in deed as the religious lobby groups wield a lot of power and influence despite a steep decline in the number of people practising any religion. The Coalition government has been pushing for a revamp of the religious discrimination laws to allow religious bodies to have special dispensation to discriminate.

Russia

Since the end of the Cold War in 1991, Russia has loomed large in Australia's foreign affairs as Australia walks a tightrope of increasing its trade with Russia but also aware of Russia's expansion plans through influencing other countries. Tony Abbott once threatened to "shirtfront" Vladimir Putin over Russian involvement in the downing of a plane and its use naval ships north of Australia. Abbott had no idea what shirtfront really meant. Putin laughed it off and Australia went down in Russian estimation. Because of our close defence ties with the US, Australia has often been drawn into issues that involve Russia.

<u>**Unemployment/Employment**</u>

Financial support for those unemployed has waned and many people are struggling. Rules on statistics have been changed and there is a steady increase in the underemployed. With a stroke of a pen, someone working one hour per week is considered employed. Newstart is an allowance given to the unemployed to support them when seeking new jobs. Those on these benefits must be actively seeking employment, even if there is none or they lose the benefits. They become easy targets for politicians and the media and named as dole bludgers. For many people particularly in rural regions there aren't jobs available and this causes an exodus to the city as it is difficult to survive on the allowance given. Australian manufacturing has all but shut down completely. There is a large amount of automation in many work places and that means that fewer people are needed. With a large pool of people to choose from, employers are able to suppress wages too. Traditional jobs gone, little change in education to expand opportunities, low wage growth and a very low unemployment benefit, young people cannot get into the job market and housing market. This just further stagnates the economy.

<u>**Unions**</u>

There has been a dramatic decline in union membership in Australia to the extent that the Labor Party, the traditional voice of the unions in parliament are losing their base and are being forced to look elsewhere. Many unions have become political and dominated by trying to achieve political ideological gains rather than act in the best interest of their members. This has led to the disenfranchisement of members and the loss of membership. However, the biggest change has been due to the Coalition government's push to undermine unions and change labour laws.

World trade

Countries and groups of nations have put in trade tariffs and barriers to protect their own producers. However, because there is a supply and demand backbone to all their economies, and multinational companies, governments have been trying to reach individual agreements between countries. Some of these are symbolic and trade can see the dumping of cheap or excess products which greatly affect an individual nation. Cheap labour in some countries undercuts others. Scarcity of one commodity can affect the capacity of another. There is no level playing field as countries try to woo individual companies with lucrative tax deals. China has entered the market and is now a powerful player and the once dominant US is finding it difficult to lose its stranglehold on world markets.

Return to Contents page